MY LIFE IN CAMPS

DURING THE WAR AND MORE

Robert S. Saito

Author's Tranquility Press
ATLANTA, GEORGIA

Copyright © 2023 by Robert Saito

All rights reserved. No part of this publication may be reproduced, distributed, or transmitted in any form or by any means, including photocopying, recording, or other electronic or mechanical methods, without the prior written permission of the publisher, except in the case of brief quotations embodied in critical reviews and certain other noncommercial uses permitted by copyright law. For permission requests, write to the publisher, addressed "Attention: Permissions Coordinator," at the address below.

Robert Saito /Author's Tranquility Press
3800 Camp Creek Pkwy SW Bldg. 1400-116 #1255
Atlanta, GA 30331, USA
www.authorstranquilitypress.com

Ordering Information:
Quantity sales. Special discounts are available on quantity purchases by corporations, associations, and others. For details, contact the "Special Sales Department" at the address above.
My Life In Camps/Robert Saito
Paperback: 978-1-961908-55-0
eBook: 978-1-961908-56-7

CONTENTS

Acknowledgements 1

Concentration Camp 3

A Relocation Center
Heart Mountain, Wyoming 15

The Beginning
1930s The Depression years 23

Old House
During the Depression years from 1938 29

Walking To School
U. S. Grant Grammar School 47

Chinatown San Jose
"Chow mein" Family dinner 51

First Christmas In Camp
Candy, nuts, and gifts 54

Activities In The Camp
Growing Up 63

Sam's Place
Drinking and Gambling in Camp 74

Shoshone River
And the protectors of River 83

Police
Police interrogation in Camp 95

Toboggan
Sharing the joy of sledding 98

Pets
Horned toads, prairie dogs, and chipmunks .. 102

Lead Me Home
Where we first began 106

Housing After Camp
1945 - 1950 Substandard living spaces 111

Learn The Traditions
Traditions and cultures must be kept alive.... 123

Summer Vacation
It is now harvest time 135

Our Own House
Our parents' dream comes true 146

Pioneer
Nobujiro Saito 150

Sam Shunji Saito
1899-1969 156

Yayeko Saito
December 1913 - April 1999 167

Acknowledgements

I thank my parents, Sam, and Yayeko Saito, for my existence and outlook on life, and my youngest brother, Julian, for making it possible for me to write short stories and get them published. All have now passed on, leaving us with beautiful and wonderful life experiences. Sterling Warner of Evergreen Valley College has encouraged me to write time and time again. My five sisters, along with my brother, who were in camp with me experiencing their own life with friends of their own age. They are part of these stories. My nieces and nephews need to know our stories because it is part of their history. I thank my wife, Naida, for allowing me the time to write without complaints.

Concentration Camp

It is an assembly center.

War starts on December 7, 1941, with the roar of Japanese bomber and fighter planes attacking Pearl Harbor. Father destroys all his gun stocks, including a shortwave set which was not used because we have no electricity, and buries the whole lot in the back yard. FBI or government agents come to the house and ask my father to produce all his weapons and the shortwave set. How did they know that father has all these items? The government agents also took some of our community leaders who were born in Japan to a jail somewhere.

I still attend school, but things are not the same, and the teacher still tries to correct my poor English. Why is this? I was born fifty miles from here and never traveled further than fifty miles from San Jose all my eight years of life. I have a strong accent. Also, since I am so thin from almost dying by eating hard, crispy pickles after a tonsil operation, which cut the inside of my throat, I have been picked on by some of my classmates and neighbors. Being skinny and talking with a strong accent is a rough life as a child, especially in school.

A small Filipino man, no taller than I at the age of eight, comes up to me near our house and glares at me. He reaches into his pocket and pulls out a knife, opens it, and threatens me with it. He looks hideous, with his dark, pockmarked face full of hate, and I turn tail and run home. What is this world coming to where an adult threatens an unarmed boy with a knife?

Within weeks after December 7, 1941, Japan's attack on Pearl Harbor, United States federal agents arrest, jail, and send alien Japanese community leaders to an undisclosed concentration camp. These men are kept separated from their families during the Second World War. All their mail is censored, personal and private life are violated, as a third party opens and reads letters, even love letters.

On February 19, 1942, President Franklin D. Roosevelt signs Executive Order 9066, restricting Japanese and Americans of Japanese descent on the West Coast of the United States to "...prescribe(d) military zones from which the movements of designated persons might be restricted or shown necessary, even excluded." We cannot live in California, because it suddenly becomes a military zone from which we are excluded. Our first move, with a minimum of advance notice, is to an "Assembly Center" at Santa Anita Racetrack in Southern California. Many barracks are hurriedly constructed for housing of the so-called designated persons, us Americans of Japanese descent. The country is in total hysteria, and all Japanese, regardless of citizenship, are suspect of being an enemy.

It is spring, 1942. I am eight years old and the oldest of seven children. We carry all our household effects and personal gear a distance of half a block to the Japanese Community Gymnasium for storage. Hundreds of people swarm in to pack their personal belongings and household goods to the ceiling for God knows how long.

Confusion and anxiety are felt by everyone because we do not know where we are going, nor what we will be able to bring with us. The talk is that we all are going to a prisoner of war camp. This could not be, because we here in California and other West Coast states are not participating in a war against America. We are Americans, not the enemy of the United States. This should not be happening to U.S. citizens. What can we do to fight this crime against U.S. citizens?

The day comes when we are herded and transported from Japanese Town to the San Jose train station. The whole family, my parents, granduncle Nobujiro, and seven pre-adolescent children are carrying what clothes we can. That is about all that we can manage. Ted is the youngest at one year old and must be carried. The last- minute notice given to us does not prepare for a move such as this. They are taking us children away from classmates who are our friends. One, two, three, etc., we take a family count and board a train to the concentration camp, or as they call it, an "assembly center."

Finally, we arrive at Santa Anita Camp, according to the orders of the United States government and General Dewitt. We have traveled some four hundred miles south from San Jose, California. Barbed-wire fences and guard towers with armed soldiers surround the camp, a very impressive sight. Armed soldiers dressed in olive drab wool uniforms, steel helmets, leggings, and brightly shined boots guard the camp with rifles and bayonets attached, ready for action. Does the United States government think our family are dangerous enemies? We are now prisoners of war, regardless of our age, and detained because we are American of Japanese ancestry. This is a concentration camp.

Escorted by armed soldiers, we all get off the train. One, two, three... all here. Another count is taken of our family. We children are following our parents and granduncle, making sure that we all are together. We are home in Santa Anita, California. Santa Anita means Saint Anne in Spanish. Saint Anne is the mother of Saint Mary, who is the mother of Jesus Christ. But this place is a famous racetrack where people wager on horses. Gambling even took place two thousand years ago, and dice were thrown to find who would win Jesus's tunic when he was crucified. There will be no horseracing while we are here, just people looking at the soldiers who are looking at us in a concentration camp. Does anyone comprehend what is happening here currently? It is so unreal.

We are all assigned family numbers; ours is 32418; this will be our family number if the war is on. Numbers become our identity, dehumanizing us. Prisoners are given numbers, and names are not used. So far, all our immediate family are together and sleeping in barracks, two rooms next to each other, except Granduncle Nobujiro, who is housed elsewhere because he is considered a bachelor.

Inside the racetrack camp, there are rows upon rows of horse stables for the less-fortunate internees, assigned to them as berthing areas. However, they are clean and do give shelter. This shelter is a stable, just like Christ's family had in their time of need.

The fortunate ones, including our family, are housed in the rows of newly constructed black tar-papered barracks on top of fresh asphalt foundations. Everything is black, and when the sun shines, it gets hot, and the smell of heated tar surrounds the barracks and us. The asphalt softens in the heat. The sun is shining constantly in Southern California, and when it doesn't, the moon shines and the spotlight that the soldiers use from the guard towers lights up the camp.

Our new home, a barracks, is furnished with folding cots and white sacks which are washed and dried in the hot Southern California sun with the rest of the laundry. Blankets are hung out to air weekly. Later in the afternoon, the sack is filled with fresh dry straw and placed on the cot. The mattress is shaken and pounded to evenly distribute the straw, to be free from uncomfortable lumps and bare spots. The smell of fresh straw is comforting, but I really prefer sleeping on a regular mattress, and it does not have to be a goose down mattress.

I'm sure the people sleeping in the stables are given cots and sack full of fresh straw, like us. It would be horrible if they had to sleep on the bare straw like the horses that were once housed there. Is there a smell of the horses remaining in the stalls, or have the authorities fumigated them all? Are the huge black horseflies still occupying these spaces and buzzing annoyingly loudly near their ears, keeping everyone awake?

Occasionally the canvas cots are scrubbed, washed clean, and dried in the sun. There is so much cleanliness here in the camp that pests will have a difficult time surviving, especially when the strong, dark brown lye soap is used. This soap is supposed to kill germs and small pests like mites, lice, fleas, and bedbugs. The smell of the soap alone will drive the pests away.

The communal toilets are separated into men's and women's, naturally, with showers and wash basins. The most striking aspect of the restroom is that it is roomy, with lots of fresh air. We really need that in the restroom, you know, especially when so many people are crowded in the camp. There is absolutely no privacy here. The truth of nakedness and the smell of humanity cannot be hidden. The toilet paper is so soft that I don't have to crumple it up to soften it like I used to in San Jose.

The water is hot when it comes out from the tap for washing my face and for the showers, unlike the old man's house. That old house had a cold water tap and we had to heat water in large pots on the cast-iron wood-burning stove. They even have flushing toilets and electric light bulbs to light up the area, which is much brighter than the gas lamps we had in San Jose. We are now living in the twentieth century, unlike the old Stone Age Sacamano house in San Jose.

Family laundry is done outdoors in a long, shallow wooden trough with water faucets every few feet, so many people can wash with individual washboards at one time. This laundry area is a social gathering place for many mothers. Daily news and gossip are passed on here. Men do not gather here for gossip, but they have to wash their clothes here if they are single. It is difficult to scrub by hand with the lye soap, because it makes the hands very slippery.

Mother loses her wedding ring here; we all look very hard until dark, but with no success. This gold ring was to be part of the family's wealth, but now, aside from the few dollars we have, the only other asset is my father's wedding ring, a half-carat diamond ring, and a gold pocket watch with chain.

Many families wear their jewelry, so it won't be stolen from the hand-carried luggage during the search for contraband by government officials. The best way to carry assets, aside from cash, is to wear them as jewelry, like gold and precious stones, but hidden. Paper money has been sewn into the garments to hide it. People who are rich and have lots of dollars converted it into jewelry, gold, and gems. The search party will have to harm the wearer of the jewelry when they try to remove it from the body. As the old saying goes, "over my dead body."

There are so many people at this assembly center that everyone is given a colored mess hall card and must go to a particular place and time for their meals. It will be impossible to feed everyone in one mess hall at the same time. The line is long for all the meals, but then we all have plenty of time to stand in line; what else is there to do? Watching the armed guards outside the barbed-wire fence is so boring. Once inside, sitting down to eat, the noise of the crowd chatting and laughing brings the atmosphere to a different level of elated emotion. Unlike the somber mood, looking at the bare walls of the room in the barracks, people are now getting to know their fellow internees, if only briefly over a hot meal and coffee.

One day, there is a big gathering inside the camp, near the main gate. I ran there and looked out from the barbed-wire fence. Soldiers are standing outside with their rifles and bayonets, ready for action. The large crowd inside the camp yelled and screamed at the soldiers. Not really understanding the full scope of my imprisonment, I give support by yelling and shaking my fist and giving them a single-digit salute like the rest of the adults, but not knowing what it means. I feel brave and safe from harm on this side of the fence. Would they really shoot us? We are unarmed and can't go any farther than the fence. Are we so dangerous that we must be imprisoned? Why am I doing this? Aren't all children supposed to be joyful beings? It was fun and exhilarating doing this anyway.

That evening, armed squads of soldier's patrol inside the camp. This routine continues for weeks. Soldiers and government officials search for contraband and confiscate scissors and knives. Now, soldiers feel safe because the women can't attack them with dangerous weapons. Of course, the women can't sew now. Talk is that money and jewelry are being stolen by the officials searching for the contraband.

I wonder how many of our men steal table knives from the mess halls and sharpen them for personal knives. One steals from other thieves. Men are sharpening table knives on stones. Japanese men love knives, especially samurai swords. They must have an inborn habit of sharpening steel for cutting things.

The young men feel oppressed, with their freedom taken away, and helpless because they are imprisoned with family members, unable to do anything about it. Afraid that the soldiers will harm their parents and family if they revolt, the young men spend days and days of wandering around the camp like rats in a cage, talking to other men of their same age, building up their hatred for being imprisoned because they are Japanese Americans. They finally take to the street and to the main gate to start a protest. These men are desperate, seeing no future for themselves or for their families, and believe that they must do something. They foresee no savior coming to assist them in saving themselves.

Many of us were born here in the United States. Most of us speak English; most of us are educated here, but the problem is that many Americans don't think we are Americans. Some of the Japanese Americans feel rejected by Americans, but where can we go? The Japanese in Japan think our "chi" (soul or blood) is tainted. All citizens are Americans, but still, racial discrimination is practiced in the United States, more so with the multicultural Americans.

The riot stopped quickly. What can they do when the soldiers have weapons and the young men have just a dream of freedom? There is no deep hatred from the past to kindle their desire to protest further. The immigrants came to this fine country of opportunity to prosper and begin a new life. Nisei, the next generation, born to the immigrants, were for the most part brought up as Americans and to love this land as their own. Sansei, children of Nisei, have absolutely no ties to Japan, and are fully committed Americans, so they cannot understand why Americans are imprisoning other Americans just because they look different. There is just confusion and despair, but no deep hatred from the past that brought this riot about. It is just a spontaneous happening that could not have been stopped.

There are no suicide bombers carrying explosives to charge the barbed-wire fence, to blast a hole for the rest to escape, like the ones we heard of during the Japanese fighting against the Chinese in the 1930s. This type of suicide warfare was glorified and condoned by Japan. Suicide is not an option, because there is simply no future in it. The mothers suffer greatly from this loss, so why do young men do these things for the glory of the nation or God? Soldiers here at Santa Anita are bewildered at the action of the rioters. The armed soldiers show no taunting or aggression toward us. We are the brave ones because we are protected by the barbed-wire fence that they built for us.

Work is going on for the war effort. Huge nettings are strung on the grandstand area of the racetrack, and adults and children weave colored strips of cloth between the netting to make camouflage. I stand on the grandstand seat and work as hard as anyone else and feel very proud to help weave the colored strips of cloth into the webbing. We are angry for being in the camp but help with the war effort. After all, we are Americans. Many camouflage nettings are being made here in the grandstand of the Santa Anita Racetrack. This camouflage will hide our military arsenals and equipment from enemy airplanes called the Zeros and Mitsubishi.

For exercise, I walk around the racetrack with the older people, rather than the younger ones, because I'm still recuperating and weak from an injury, I suffered last year. The track with the soft dirt is ideal for anyone who walks. Just as in the military and school, most participate in the daily exercise of stretching and bending early in the morning in front of the barracks just before breakfast. This loosens the muscles and makes for fewer aches and keeps everyone physically fit and alert. The elders get the children to practice with them. They chant the count: *ichi, ni, san, shi, ichi, ni, san, shi* and on and on, one, two, three, four. Are we getting physically fit to fight a war in case it comes to the camp? For many of the elderly, this exercise has been performed daily for years, and they do not plan to give up being physically fit. No wonder they live to be old. The elders want us younger people to get into the routine of physical fitness they have been practicing for years.

In August 1942, families are moved out to different camps throughout the United States. Father's mother, who lived in "Little Tokyo" Los Angeles, and his younger brother Seiki (Tom), who lived and worked at Loyola Marymont University, a Catholic University in Los Angeles, are sent to Manzanar Camp, California, near a town called Independence. How ironic, a town with the name of Independence is near a concentration camp. Manzanar War Relocation Center houses many people from Southern California. Uncle Seiki was a cook at the university, preparing meals for the university staff and students. Will Uncle Seiki become a cook at the Manzanar camp?

Our family is transferred from the assembly center at Santa Anita to a "War Relocation Center" at Heart Mountain, Wyoming. There are other camps, named Tule Lake, California; Poston I and II, Arizona; Gila, Arizona, etc. Each camp holds about ten thousand internees.

Our family is transferred from the assembly center at Santa Anita to a "War Relocation Center" at Heart Mountain, Wyoming. There are other camps, named Tule Lake, California; Poston I and II, Arizona; Gila, Arizona, etc. Each camp holds about ten thousand internees.

Approximately 120,000 people of Japanese descent are relocated to the camps. We are locked away by the federal government, who think we may be spies for a foreign country that most of us have no ties with. The federal government is afraid that we may turn against our homeland, the United States. How wrong they are! We are herded onto the train to begin our journey to God-knows-where, to places we have never heard of before. No one tells children anything. One, two, three... all the family including Granduncle Nobujiro is on board, traveling together again, carrying the few possessions we have. How confusing; a lot of rapid. moves since March of this year. We are going further away from where we used to live. At least the family is together.

A Relocation Center
Heart Mountain, Wyoming

We are on our way to Heart Mountain, Wyoming, a relocation center for us to last the duration of the war. At least the immediate family is together. We have left our classmates behind at San Jose, and newfound friends of five months at Santa Anita camp.

The conductor gives everyone salt tablets when we are crossing the Sonoran Desert of Arizona. It is hot, HOT! It is the end of August and the beginning of September in Southern California and the Arizona desert. The wheels of the train go clickity-clack, clickity-clack as they roll over the gap between the rails. The hot sun beats down on the metal roofs, and the interior becomes an oven, a living inferno. All the windows are open, but the heat can't be driven away. It is terrible. It feels like Purgatory. Thirsty! I'm so thirsty I could drink a gallon of ice water in one gulp. The water is warm, almost hot. A wet towel against the face is the only way to keep cool. The hot white sand with sparse vegetation does not make the desert ride any cooler.

Now the train is taking us out of Purgatory into cooler places in the higher elevations, and the train windows must be closed to keep the warmth inside. How can it change from an oven to an icebox overnight? Mother says we have traveled through four seasons of the year within the several days it took to get to Heart Mountain, Wyoming on September 4, 1942. Now winter is here, or seems to be, by the look and feel of things.

I can't believe there are patches of white snow on the dark ground. The wind is making it colder. One, two, three... we are all here in Heart Mountain. I was given a thick black wool navy pea coat. This pea coat is too big for me, with the shoulders sagging and sleeves extending well beyond my fingers, but it does keep me warm like a big blanket. I'll eventually grow into them, but how soon? They should issue me some wool underwear along with the pea coat. Even bright red long johns will be accepted just to keep warm from this bone-chilling cold.

The camp is surrounded by barbed-wire fence, and armed soldiers are in guard towers. The federal government knows that we will stay put, because they have assigned only 150 soldiers to watch over 10,000 of us. Why escape? Have you ever been to Wyoming? You wouldn't want to leave the warm shelter they call a barracks just to go for a short stroll. No one will help us escape, and we have nowhere to go. It is too cold, and we have no adequate clothing to protect ourselves from the elements.

Of the 150 soldiers, I wonder how many are on duty in the towers that watch over the camp. Do they have stoves to keep them warm? The wind must be even colder up on the guard towers.

This is our country, where we were born, and where we wish to die, so we all will stay in the camp. No one wants to fight the cold wind blowing the white snow into your face, so you can't see the huge tumbleweed coming at you full force. This is an entirely new country we have been sent to. We are being punished for what we look like and for who we are, not for what we have done.

Hot supper and a hot shower after the long, tiring train ride are welcomed. The potbellied stove is finally lit after many tries. It would have been easier to get several hot embers from the boiler room and use them as a starter. We learn as we live day by day. It doesn't take long to warm the small room. Finally, everyone is in bed, warming up under the wool blankets. Sleep comes rapidly, but it is soon interrupted.

The first night in camp is different from any other night I have ever experienced. The howling wakes me up. The sounds of wild dogs outside keep getting louder and closer. I cover my head under the blankets. Are the soldiers using wild dogs to keep us in camp at night? The howling stops and there is dead silence for the longest time. Did the dogs leave? Crash, bang, yelps, the dogs are here in camp by the mess hall, not sixty feet away! They knock the garbage cans over and fight over the food. The wild dogs are coyotes that come to visit our mess hall for food.

I am told that coyotes are cowards and will run off if yelled at or hit by a stone thrown at them. What a relief to learn that they are more afraid of us than we are of them. Still, I sleep with my head under the blankets, not because of the howling, but because of the cold nights of Wyoming. I like to sleep with my ears warm—not that I have big ears.

The night visitors eventually quit coming into camp, because each mess hall employee learns to secure the cans so the coyotes can't get at the food, even if the cans are knocked over. The garbage is needed to feed the hogs of the neighboring farmers, and the hogs and chickens the camp has. Coyotes can be heard in the distance every night, but I haven't been able to see any and don't know what they look like, nor do I care at this time.

Before entering our quarters, there is a mud room or hallway between the two rooms. This mud room is where we leave our dirty shoes and heavy clothing. Rooms E and F are assigned to our family, number 32418, in a long barracks, number sixteen, with black tar paper on the outside walls, held in place by slats nailed to the walls and roof. Fortunately, the interior wall is not papered with black tar paper, so the natural color of the wood is pleasant. It is one of many barracks for ten thousand of us.

Room E is for Mother and us, and Room F is for father. Our room is large enough for iron-framed cots to extend from both sides of the wall, head to toe, leaving an aisle in the center. In Room E, two cots, side by side, are made into a large bed where we can share blankets. Eight cots are placed together to make four double beds. Two pairs of cots are put in the far corners of the room to economize space. The other pair is alongside the corner cots, with a very small aisle between them, leaving a large space between the cots and a large potbellied cast-iron stove, the only other furnishing in this room. It is so bare that it is cold in the room and the wood floor with open knotholes doesn't help.

Windows in the back wall and in the front wall allow sunlight into the room. A drop cord lights the room with a light bulb in the center of the room. Is a prison cell any different? Whoever is first to rise before sunrise stokes the stove and places more coal inside to heat the room. I have a habit of bearing myself behind to warm up faster. Once I back up too much and my bare bottom hits the hot stove. Pssss! For weeks, I can't sit or sleep on my back. The pain is bad, and it is embarrassing, especially eating standing up in the mess hall, but it is more comfortable than sitting.

The windows are covered with a cloth, not to give us privacy, but for insulation purposes for now; but later, there will be regular catalog-purchased curtains with bright colors. Otherwise, the ice-cold windows will radiate the freezing temperature into the small room. The knotholes, especially the floorboards, are covered with tin can tops nailed over them. This prevents the cold from entering the room. At least now we have better shelter and warmth.

Each block is divided into two sections: lower and upper blocks. We live in an upper block closest to Heart Mountain to the north. In the center of each half block, there is an H-shaped building containing the boiler room in the center, with a large storage bin for coal for a large boiler and our potbellied stoves. One leg of the H has toilets, washbasins, and shower rooms for women on one end, the north side, and for men on the south side. The other leg of the H is the laundry room and drying room on the east side. Although we are known to be honest and trustworthy, personal property such as clothing, including socks and underwear, are never dried in this room. The drying room does not have clotheslines strung, nor is it warm enough for the clothes to dry. These precious clothing items are dried in our barracks room, near the warm potbellied stove. They are hung, but not secured, with a clothespin. Buying clothespins is an extra expense.

The mess hall is in the northern part of the block, next to the H-shaped building. It serves over a hundred people three times a day. Eating utensils are the heavy stainless-steel U.S. Army-issue knives, forks, and large spoons. A heavy, stainless-steel tray with sections is our so-called plate, and when that is not used, a large, thick, shallow bowl is filled with rice, etc. A very thick, heavy mug is our cup, and a very thick, heavy bowl is for soup or breakfast cereal.

The cereal is usually hot rolled oats or grits on which we pour cream from a small tin can with a flower label, Carnation brand, and add some sugar. Dry cereal is offered, but hard to consume with cold milk when the weather is so cold outside. Chopsticks are allowed if we don't use them as weapons. (Just kidding.) We do not have to be told to eat everything that is on our metal tray, because everyone takes just what they need and no more. Conservation is the rule. The old saying and rule is: "Eat all your food because there are starving children in China."

The meals at the mess hall are called by one of the kitchen helpers, who strikes a steel rod shaped into a triangle with a metal rod. This is what I call "chow call on a chow bell." The breakfast is often fresh eggs with rice, or hotcakes and syrup. Coffee is given to me, even though I am a young boy. A hot cup of coffee is enjoyed with lots of condensed milk from a can and several teaspoons of sugar to sweeten it. Father used to forbid us from eating sweets of all kinds because it destroys the teeth, but now he is not around to discipline me on the usage of sugar. Isn't that great? I have more freedom in the camp now than I had before at home.

Lunch and supper are served with lots of potatoes or rice with stew or gravy. The variety is here so we won't be tired of eating the same thing day after day. My brother Ted and sister Mary hate egg foo yung, because they say it is served all the time. Well, they must get rid of all the eggs the chickens lay. No wonder they didn't like egg foo yung; there wasn't any soy sauce. I like it and they can feed it to us more often, as far as I'm concerned. It is like an omelet, but it has more different varieties of vegetables. Can you imagine how many eggs are used to feed 10,000 internees? How many hens are at work? The only food that I cannot stand is cream soup.

While in the Santa Clara County Hospital last year, they served me cream of tomato soup, and all the vegetable cream soups they can cook up and think of. A boy can take only so many cream soups. The cooks do have Jell-O occasionally, which the hospital did serve me occasionally, which I like. Ice cream is something the camp cooks did not make, which was also served occasionally in the hospital. I sure do miss ice cream. The Japanese just have not learned how to make ice cream at home, therefore they don't know how at this mess hall. It was the first and last time I have tasted the wonderful treat called ice cream, in the County Hospital at San Jose, California.

Gravy on potatoes, gravy on rice, or gravy on bread (often call chipped beef on toast for breakfast, or SOS), are the comfort foods that I liked, and they do serve it quite often. I am too young to know what SOS means, and the cooks won't tell me. We are fed well, and many of the people in this camp are now complaining about the food, while the rest of the nation is on rations for butter and sugar, but then there are always the complainers who are not happy with any situation, whether good or bad. They don't have to cook it or wash the trays, and they complain about this easy life. Jiminy Crickets! I say "Jiminy Crickets" a lot, because it is better than using bad words, which so far are not taught to me.

Rumors have it that horse meat is served instead of beef. I cannot tell the difference. Red meat is seldom served, except in stew and soup.

The cooks get up early in the morning to have all the breakfast ready when the sun comes up, and the scullery people clean and wash the mess gear, the kitchen, and the eating area. These mess hall workers love to scrub the floors every day with soap and water. The complainers go back to their rooms and complain some more, while warming themselves by the potbellied stove about not being able to farm like they used to, while the rest of the nation is suffering from a coal and fuel shortage. Did they forget that farming is a hard life, with lots of physical labor from sunup to sundown, and not making money at it and often starving? They never had it so good, as my parents would say.

__The Beginning__
1930s The Depression years

This is what I remember when I was a baby. I'm looking up while lying in a crib and the fresh breeze is blowing across my face, at the same time, moving the leaves of the aspen tree above me. The leaves are dark on one side, light on the other, and the cool breeze flutters these leaves from dark to light, often showing the blue sky above. Try as I might, I cannot touch the beautiful leaves. The aspen leaves are my mobile, and I am happy. To be in the shade of the aspen tree with the leaves fluttering is to be in heaven.

Aspen Tree

*Aspen tree wakens
to soft gentle breeze blowing
saying I'm alive.*

I also remember crawling on the farmhouse's wooden floor. My parents and I sleep on the floor, so I don't remember ever falling out of a bed or a crib. Sleeping on a straw mat called a tatami is a Japanese custom and is cheaper than buying a bed, box springs, and mattress. A comforter is called a futon, and we do not sleep on a futon. The farmhouse is near a small village called Berryessa, California, where there is a general store and a gas station. The gas station sells kerosene for lamps and stoves.

My father often removes a couple of wooden floorboards and puts or removes things in the hole beneath, usually taking a swig from a large bottle during the process. After a long, hot day of working, supper, hot bath, and a drink of sake is heaven.

These are the things I remember when I was a baby and roaming around the farm between the rows of broccoli. There is a farmhouse where I visit a Mexican boy my age, living with his parents. He is my only playmate because my sisters are too young. I love to walk around the other farms as well.

One day, a young Japanese American couple living close by our farm finds me in a ditch near a main road some distance from home. They cannot wake me up, so they take me to their house and wipe my hot face with a cool, wet towel. Later, when I awaken, they send me home. They tell my mother that I must have fainted in the heat of the day, so they took me home. Some people call this a sunstroke. I have often wondered if this has caused any damage to my brain.

There is a bunkhouse where several Filipino-American men live. They are the farmhands that my father hires at twenty-five to thirty cents per hour. A contract is signed, keeping everything legal. These are hard times, and work is difficult to find because of the influx of migrant workers from other states and Mexico. The farmers around my father's farm hire these Filipino-American men first, because they are hard workers, punctual, and live close by. Sometimes, migrant workers do not show up for work the day after payday or on Mondays, because they lie in bed, trying to get rid of the terrible headache that was acquired the day before. Many Asians do not enjoy drinking alcohol, except a few Japanese like my father. The Filipino-American men would rather go to the dime-a- dance hall in Chinatown and enjoy female company. Can you blame them?

It is difficult to understand why Filipino Americans work in long, dark raincoats, bandannas covering the head-neck area, and a wide-brim straw hat. Naturally, they wear shirts, trousers, cotton gloves, socks, and boots. Father tells me that all those clothes are to protect them from the heat of the burning sun and to keep them from dehydrating. The cotton gloves have the fingertips cut off to feel the work they must do. In other words, these men are covered from head to toe, except a small portion of their face and fingertips. It is as if the sun's rays will turn them into dust, as it does to a vampire from Transylvania.

Deer do come down from the hills and mountain into the foothills farm area to eat the delicious vegetables growing so young and tender. Father carries his .30-30 rifle during the deer season while farming the land, and his .22 caliber rifle when rabbits start to lay waste to his vegetable crop. When a rabbit is spotted, whistle and the rabbit will sit up and listen to find the direction of the shrill noise. This few second of curiosity enables a hunter to bead in on a rabbit, and it will soon be stew meat. Either way, this is one way of getting meat on the table. Really, I don't remember eating venison, but I do remember eating rabbits.

Rabbits

Rabbits eat wary,
Always alert for danger,
Will never tarry.

During the winter months, when he has more time for recreation, Father goes fishing, using his special split bamboo pole and an expensive reel. His dream is to catch the biggest striped bass and the largest steelhead trout in California, but he does bring home enough other fish to feed all of us, including neighbors and the Filipino field hands living in the bunkhouse.

It is very dangerous carrying a weapon anytime. Guns are made to kill. People do target practice, but this is only to perfect their killing skills. It is not easy taking aim on a prey and shooting it. There are factors like wind, distance, and movement of the prey.

Farmers have been found dead from gunshot wounds in and around this area. One Japanese-American farmer was found with a head wound and his weapon lying on the other side of the fence. People are wondering whether he took his own life, because times are very difficult since the fall of the stock market and the Depression, or if it was an accident.

Another Japanese American was killed because the weapon exploded on him. It was an accident because of carelessness. He laid his gun down barrel-first, and found that the dirt clogged the barrel, so he decided to shoot the dirt out, and the boom went the barrel.

These years in California, Asians are not allowed to own property, so Father must sharecrop or be a tenant farmer. In fact, we are not allowed to attend public schools. This is the land of opportunity, they say; yes, it is, for the rich landowners, but my father still has hopes of eventually becoming a person with property, and raising a large family to take care of him and my mother when they get old.

My mother is getting tired of being a farmer's wife, living on the edge financially, not knowing when total loss will come. She goes out at night to cut broccoli so we can have something to eat the next day. Mother hates broccoli because of this. We have other vegetables growing around the farmhouse. There are string beans, white radishes, eggplants, burdock, and other vegetables to cook. Father always buys a one- year supply of new crop rice by the one-hundred-pound sacks to last one year.

Father has hot beds with canvas tops for protection against frost to his tomato plants. He has thrown in his chips on tomatoes for the season. It is a great gamble because he is now completely broke, depending on these small plants to produce a bumper crop for the season. The plants still need protection because of the early spring killing frost. Soon the Filipino-American farmhands will transplant these tomato plants to the farmland.

Our family's German shepherd dog, Bobby, chases a rabbit and tears the canvas top off the hothouses and ruins the season's tomato plants. The frost kills all the plants, and father's credit rating is so bad that he has to quit farming and get a city job fast. The rabbit is dead, Bobby is dead, and Father feels like he is dead holding his weapon. It is a very sad day and there is nothing else to do but to pull up the stakes, move to the city, and find a job.

Mother is so young, with several children to take care of; her life now has changed drastically from dire need living in poverty as a farmer's wife to an uncertainty of a darker life of poverty in a city where she has no friends. There is a bright side now she is no longer a farmer's wife eating broccoli. Mother is now a wife with an unemployed husband, five children, and Uncle Nobujiro, living in a very old and cold house. A Christian church comes to the rescue with food staples and clean clothes.

Father finds a job as a janitor at Hale Brothers Department Store in downtown San Jose, California. He will have a steady paycheck coming in during these Depression years. Another happy surprise is that mother is pregnant with Mary, due to give birth in December of 1938. This gives my parents six children to assist them into old age.

__Old House__
During the Depression years from 1938

We moved into an old wooden house that survived many years of adverse weather to where all reminiscence of paint has long disappeared. The tall fence that protects the property is also weathered and devoid of paint if it has ever been painted at all. The shingled roof needs repairs, but it is noticeable only during the rainy season, when rainwater drops into metal pots and pails placed below the leaks, reminding us that patching is needed.

There is an artistic beauty in this old house, with the spring growth of green leaves on the fruit trees, and grapevines climbing and winding through the arbor leading from the front gate to the rear of the house. The covered porch is well-worn from years of traffic from the front yard leading to the entrance. The dirt has an abrasive effect on the wood. Only the street is paved.

The old man, who owns the house, lives in a dilapidated shack in the back alongside the large red- brick building of the pottery next door. Between the house and his shack is a vintage outhouse without plumbing. Alongside the shack are lean-tos which house smelly goats, noisy chickens, and quiet mice. A barn with a hoist to lift bales of hay up to the loft is located across from the lean-tos. I have never witnessed any hay being lifted on to the loft but have observed hay being lowered for hungry goats.

The old man pushes his two-wheeled cart daily to various markets, restaurants, canneries, and packing houses, to gather old fruits and vegetable trimmings and other foods which goats, chickens, and even he himself eat. They are all better fed than many people during these Depression years of the late 1930s.

The old man is self-sufficient, having long ago emigrated from Italy and finally settled in San Jose, California. His needs are minimal. He has some trimmings from his cart that can be eaten, goat milk for nourishment and cheese, chicken, and eggs for meat. Eggs and chickens are also sold for flour, salted fat back, salt, and other items which are needed from time to time. He may be trading his eggs and chickens for fresh fish or other goods being sold by traveling salespersons who come by the house. This is the bartering system of long ago.

An arbor supporting grapevines furnishes enough fruit to make wine for his personal use. The old man can make wine from grapes and fruits that grocers throw away daily. The old man is weathered and bent over, usually pushing a cart slowly to and from the house, but he must be healthy, eating vegetables and fruits and drinking his daily glasses of wine and goat milk. He is from a generation that shuns water because it has sickened and killed many during his lifetime. I doubt he uses water to bathe and wash clothes. Wine and goat milk are safer than water to drink.

If water must be consumed, it is boiled with coffee, tea, or herbs to flavor it.

It is difficult to even guess his age because of the stubble of white hairs which covers his wrinkled sunburned face. His clothing is old and worn as well, with no proof that it has ever been washed with soap and water. It shines with layers of dirt and grime, and this may act as insulation from the cold weather and holds the fabric together. There are many people, hobos, Dust Bowl families, and migrants, who have only three sets of clothing or less. One for daily use, another when the other is being washed and dried, and the third is their Sunday-go-to-meeting clothes.

The old man's thick, heavy boots are dirty and have seen many years of service. The cobbler or he himself must have replaced the soles and heels many times. Father has a set of shoe repairing tools in the cellar, which includes cast-iron stands to hold shoes or boots in place while heels or soles are being replaced and nailed. Footwear is expensive; therefore, they must be repaired when possible to save money. Shoes are made from thick cow hides, so they can weather the wear and tear of walking on the many unpaved walkways and alleys or even streets in most cities.

The old man is from a time of the late 1800s and surviving the same way. This type of person is a survivor from a different age, who has seen hard times often and takes each day as a challenge in life. His journey into this life has surely been a long and interesting one. He takes each day at a time, not knowing exactly what tomorrow brings and caring less, because he has already laid away his survival kit for the worst that may come.

This old house has no modern convenience except natural gas for heating a small standing-off-the-floor furnace in the living room, and gas lamps located in each room for illumination. Natural gas pipes jut out from the walls. The mantle from the end of the gas pipe is lit at night, and the light is bright enough to read, if you are within a few feet from it. The only other modern item is a cold-water spigot in the kitchen sink. The walls are covered with intricate designed wallpaper.

Our stove is a large cast-iron wood burner. There is always a large pot of hot soup or stew available for anyone who needs food, which includes hobos who stop by for nourishment. They have marked the back of our fence which runs along the railroad tracks. I really don't know what kind of marking they have put on the fence, because it is hard to find. Often, dumplings are added by Granduncle Nobujiro, and I can tell you that it is delicious and filling. Granduncle Nobujiro always gives the hobos a large bowl of food and a big chunk of sourdough bread baked in the oven of our cast-iron stove. The hobos do rake the yard for their meal if the yard need raking. Sometimes it is raked more than once a day during the autumn.

Our cast-iron stove is used to heat water for bathing and laundry. Hot water is poured into a large, galvanized tub and the washing starts, for clothing or body, whichever needs to be washed for the day. After the clothes are starched and dried, Mother heats several irons on the stove and irons the clothing, and often sprinkles water onto the clothes by alternating the irons. Is this another way of saying "having more than one iron on the fire?" Everyone in the family is happy having nice, crisp, starched clothes to wear. At least the diapers aren't starched and ironed.

The first floor has the dining and kitchen area as one room in the rear, and the living room and the main bedroom are in the front. The main bedroom is where Father's uncle lives because he has a hard time climbing stairs. Up a narrow and steep stairway are two bedrooms on the second floor. The front bedroom is where my parents sleep with the youngest child, Mary. I share the back bedroom bed with my other four sisters.

There are two varieties of fig trees growing along the south side the house, and two varieties of apricot trees growing in the front yard facing west. As mentioned before, the arbor with grapevines has several varieties of grapes. The back fence has prickly pear cacti growing alongside, which deters anyone scaling the wooden fence to steal chickens, eggs, or even a goat.

Times are hard, you know, but no one is interested in stealing prickly pears or the cactus leaves. I like the prickly pears but find them seedy, and if you get past the sharp needles, it is truly a delicious experience. The best way to get to the meat of the cactus pear is to cut both ends off while using leather gloves, and slice the skin from end to end, then peel the skin, leaving the sweet, delicious center full of seeds and meat.

Mexicans enjoy the young cactus leaf, which they call *nopales*. The needles are cut away, using a sharp knife and leather gloves. The tender leaves are diced and cooked with onions, tomatoes, and scrambled eggs. However, the tastiest is cooking it with chopped or diced pork instead of eggs. During the Depression, the *nopales* are cooked without eggs or meat. I love it, not the Depression, but the *nopales*. It really isn't any fun cutting away the needles. A hazardous job description for a cook indeed. At least the needles don't jump and stab you, although some believe they do.

I often climb out of the upper bedroom window onto the large white fig tree and down to the ground and eat a few figs on the way down when they are ripe. The figs are eaten with skin and all. Lots of fiber from the skin, including the many seeds inside. The old man does not want me to climb on the trees, but then, how can a person stop a pre-adolescent boy from doing anything he wants to do? He even tries to stop me from eating those sweet, ripe fruits. I don't want them to spoil on the trees or vines. He is too old to harvest them alone, and he only harvests the low-branch fruits that he can reach. Some figs are dried by his shed. I'm only helping by harvesting the ones located higher up the tree. He speaks to my father in Italian, and Father answers like they are chatting, but I know that the old man is talking about me climbing the trees and eating his fruits.

Father still dreams of catching the elusive thirty-six- inch fighting steelhead trout and striped bass. Steelhead trout looks like and has habits similar to salmon, in that they are seagoing and spawn in the same streams or rivers they were born in. The only way that I can tell the marked difference is in the tail. One has a tail that appears to be chopped at the end, and the other splits at the end. Now, Pop cannot hunt or fish because he works long hours and is without a car, but still cleans and cares for the guns and fishing gear, waiting for the time when he can go to fulfill his dream of catching the elusive game fish. After cleaning and oiling his outboard motor, he clamps it in a fifty-five-gallon steel oil drum full of clear water and test runs the motor, spewing bluish-white smoke, indicating it is all in working order, before storing it in the cellar.

Father loves to bring home what he calls *foo ryu*, a Chinese concoction of tofu marinated in Chinese rice wine and lot of salt. A small cube of this strong- flavored tofu, which must have been aging for many months if not years, buried or stored somewhere dark and mysterious, is placed on top of rice, and makes a wonderful, tasty meal.

Another meal with a bowl of hot rice is a little bit of Japanese *shio kara*, that is bits of octopus and/or squid and God knows what other parts of those animals, that has been marinated in salt for a very long time, and you can tell just by its smell, and it is very well seasoned with age. One must use very little of this in a bowl of rice with lots of green tea or water to wash it down. This is like the Filipino shrimp fry or *bagoon*. All tasty but one must get through the smell or pinch the nose closed, and all are guaranteed to draw flies from the neighborhood to the food. It does make me very thirsty and smell bad, but my belly is contented and full.

Father makes the best pickles of sliced cucumbers, onion strips, napa cabbage leaves, flakes of red chili peppers marinated in rice wine vinegar, salt, sugar, and water. He really outshines all by making his daikon radishes and cucumbers salted in a mixture of rice wine mash, which I love to eat. The mash is the leftover pulp after the rice wine has been squeezed out. It has the sharp tang of alcohol, reminding us to eat small bits of it, like sipping on rice wine.

The Depression is hard, and Father must improvise to survive, using lots of salt as a preservative because of the lack of refrigeration. If we have rice, my parents improvise with all kinds of pickles and vegetables. Father buys a new crop rice in bulk, that is sacks and sacks of one-hundred-pound bags of rice at one time, so we will have enough rice for one year. He insists on the new crop because stores will try to sell off all the old crop before selling the new crop. My parents can taste the newness of the grain and can taste the old crop. As far as I am concerned, the pickles and the other salted items that we have occasionally masks all the taste of the rice, new or old. Granduncle Nobujiro just smiles and is very content with his current life with our family because he has been eating this most of his life.

Naturally, the Japanese grocer will not give Father credit when buying, because our large family is poor, so he always pays in cash. Some of the people feel that Father is working at a job that is below dignity. They fail to realize, as Father has said many times, that any job must be done by someone, and as long as one keeps working to survive and taking care of the family, it is dignified.

A farmhand, dishwasher, and even a janitor brings in food for the table and a roof over their family's heads. If this is not enough, other members of the family can ease the burden of the breadwinner by sharing with their earnings. This is how many immigrants are surviving and saving their monies to buy homes, businesses, and even sending their children to college.

Large families such as ours are crowding into small homes; sometimes two or more families are living in one small home. This is survival, and it has been done for generations, and will continue for generations to come. There will be new immigrants to take the place of the ones who have moved on to better lives. This is part of the American dream. The ones who complain about other families living in less-than-perfect conditions have forgotten where they came from and are in denial.

Vendors of all sorts pass our street, selling ice, vegetables, eggs, milk, and even fish on ice. A rag man will come by and buy old clothes or rags. Sharpeners will sharpen almost any blade, from knives to scissors. They ring bells, sound horns, or yell out what they must sell, buy, or even barter.

Large six-to-eight-inch fresh sardines brought in from Monterey Bay are a big treat for our family, especially when Father has a few cents left over from payday. Sardines are so plentiful that the cost is cheap to feed our family with fresh charcoal-broiled fish and rice. There is an art in eating charcoal-broiled sardines. Father can pick the meat off a sardine so clean from the bones that only an intact skeletal sardine lay on the plate when he is finished. I mean that there is nothing left except bright, shining bones; not even the meat on the head or eyes are left, and this is all done with chopsticks, two pieces of sticks. The fish seem to taste best when I can do the same as Father, which is not that often. After all, he is an expert in eating sardines with chopsticks. No wonder we do not have cats living with us; there is no fish or food left for the cats to eat.

Sardines

Sardines once plenty
Like salmon in the river
Men have eaten all.

Fresh abalone is given to us by friends, and my parents do not do the sacrilegious act of cooking this delicious shellfish. They shuck the huge muscle mass from its shell and pound on it for a long time to make it tender as can be. It is sliced and laid on a platter with grated daikon surrounding it. Mother beats up some hot yellow mustard in a small ceramic bowl. When the rice is cooked to perfection, mother serves the rice in bowls for each of us. Granduncle Nobujiro will say grace, *"Ita daki mashu."* We all get our share of the abalone sashimi with the daikon on the side. A small scoop of hot mustard and a little soy sauce placed on a small plate with the abalone and a bowl of rice is our meal. This meal is fit for a king. We know that there are starving children in the world, so we do eat every portion of our meal, to the last grain of rice. Who would waste abalone sashimi?

We are a very large family, but still are clothed properly and fed normally, despite being poor during this time of hardship throughout the United States. We are not starving, nor do we wear rags for clothing. Everyone in the family wears shoes and has done so since learning to walk. Others during the Depression have gone to bed many times without food, but not our family. At least Father buys enough rice to last one year and lots of pickles of one sort or another.

My parents always give me a haircut. Father buys a hand-operated hair clipper, and many times while he clips my hair, the clipper will pull my hair. It hurts. Father pushes down on my head to keep me from moving, but all it did was make me shorter. I'm sure my parents have better things to do than cutting my hair. Mother cuts Father's and Granduncle's hair and they never fight it like me. Father has such nice black wavy hair that shines when the light hits it just right. Girls are lucky that they don't have to get a haircut, but then I would rather get a haircut than be a girl like my sisters. A very easy choice, getting a haircut, but how I hate it! Some people believe that a large bowl is placed on my head and then all the hair hanging out on the side is cut away. It may appear so, but no bowl is used. I can hardly wait until my hair grows longer and I have a normal head of hair.

Mother always sends me outdoors to play instead of being in the house with my sisters. She does not want her only son to grow up with the girls and wants me to play with the other boys in the neighborhood. Many of the Japanese American boys my age does not want to associate with me at all, except to pick on me. I avoid confrontation by staying away from their so-called turf. They don't want to play with a son whose father cleans up after other people, a father who cleans among other places, restrooms, or a mother who is deaf. It is all right, because my Italian friend across the street and I have all kinds of fun together. We even fight, but it is a fun fight with feelings hurt, but nothing of lasting memories, and the next hour is another happy time.

My Italian friend invites me over for a spaghetti dinner. They pile the food on my plate just like chow mein, with lots of sauce and cheese on top. They spin the noodles on a fork and eat it, but I, like a true Japanese, want to slurp it right up like noodle soup, but I don't. Japanese say that the more noise you make slurping the noodle into the mouth, the better the taste. It is a little sloppy but does taste good. I get a glass of red wine with the tasty pasta. I'm pre-adolescent and can't handle the wine, so I get a little tipsy. My Italian friend can handle the wine and drinks the homemade red wine with gusto. Is gusto an Italian word? It is appropriate using it here, but the wine isn't appropriate for me, who wants to slurp the noodle they call spaghetti like an old Japanese professional noodle eater.

His father built this house by himself. He is an excellent carpenter from Italy. He first builds a small one-bedroom house in the back lot, marries a young lady from across the street, and lives there while building the front main house. His father also makes several wine presses and rents them out in exchange for money or ripe grapes.

My friend and I sneak into the wine cellar and pour a glass apiece while his parents are out. The first sip, I spit it clear across the room. It is sour, I mean real sour, and I have a violent reaction to spit as far away from me as possible. Luckily, my friend was not in my line of fire. We find that it is from an oak barrel full of wine vinegar. I have no desire for any more wine or wine vinegar. This drink should be given to the hobos who sit around sipping on wine, getting drunk. It will teach them not to drink anymore, but then they might get to like it because it does have alcohol in it. During this Depression, even wine vinegar may be consumed just for the alcohol and warmth it gives.

Next door is a pottery manufacturing plant with a large fenced-in area near Jackson Street and the railroad tracks. My friend and I climb over the wooden fence along the tracks on

Sundays and run into a large barn filled with bales of straw. The straw must be used as packing material for the pottery and for fired clay bricks. They make cups, plates, bowls, and many other oven-baked household goods. It is fun to climb the bales of straw and find hiding places between them. When we hear the watchman making his rounds, we keep quiet. Then, when all is clear, we crawl through a narrow slot between the roof and wall and drop to the ground next to the railroad tracks. Another day of exciting adventure in San Jose.

Near the railroad tracks on Taylor Street is a large wooden structure where many people can sit on bleachers and watch midget car racing on a small oval. The roar of the engines, smell of exhaust, and dust is thrilling, as the small cars race around in circles to earn the prize fund. It costs fifty cents to enter. The roar vibrates my chest, and even though the cars are small, the power is felt in my small body.

Father borrows a long extension cord and strings a line from the neighbor's house to our cellar and calls our friends, including all the children who play with us, to watch his cartoons he had since the days he worked in Hollywood. The movies are reels and reels of cartoons which we watch for hours. He becomes an instant hit in the neighborhood. When he talks about his days in Los Angeles living near his parents and brother, no one really believes him, but the movies prove he had to be in Hollywood to get them.

Three of us older children go to a Christian church to learn Christianity and sing hymns. Although Mother is a Buddhist and Father is a Shinto, (his mother comes from a line of Shinto priests), they allow us to attend the Christian church. In turn, the Christian church helps our family with some staples and clothes. All this helps my parents ease themselves from the effects of the Depression that many people are suffering today.

Singing Christmas songs gets to my mother, and she sings along with my younger siblings. The one song my mother likes is "Amazing Grace" by John Newton. Even though she is very hard of hearing, she loves music and the vibration she feels. I think that the music and vibration fascinate her. She often plays a harmonica for us. The vibration of the harmonica is wonderful to hear. Deaf? Mother is not truly deaf, just hard of hearing, and she is living a normal life of motherhood; we all try not to feel her deafness, but to assist her in hearing us by speaking up so she can hear a little of our voice. She is very happy with all of us.

The Christian church opens their arms for us when our family really needed the help, when we left the farm for the city. My youngest sister is born during Christmastime, and Father names her Maria for the Virgin Mary, but with a Mexican name because of his memory spent in Mexico farming. We receive our first small bag of rock-hard Christmas candy, and my parents allow us to eat them if we share with the rest of the family. Three of us also receive our first Christmas gifts from the church.

I often wake up and see three figures in the open closet. A man, woman, and child being held are there, and I start to scream. Naturally, I'm scared when seeing something that is not supposed to be in the house. They are ghosts and no one else can see them. My parents try to calm me down. My siblings say that I'm having a nightmare, but how can it be a nightmare when I'm wide awake and seeing them in the closet? I never had these experiences at the farm, and now suddenly, these ghosts appear and only in that one spot. It is very disturbing for the family, and more so with me because I'm the only one who can see them. They are a mother and father, and a child being held in their arms. Is this an apparition of the Holy Family to watch over me?

The first time I have ever tasted the cold but sweet ice cream and Jell-O is here in this county hospital. I'm here recuperating from a tonsil operation. Soon the warmth of home and family will greet me, until I'm ready to go back to school. I ask my sister to give me some pickled radishes, which I love. Without chewing the radish well, I swallow them, and it rips open the incision and blood spews out. My sister panics and I faint, out like a light.

I have lost a lot of blood, and my parents cannot afford to buy blood, so Mother, who recently gave birth to my brother Ted, gives me one pint, which saves me. Somehow, my father could not give me blood, maybe from his illness or incompatible match. This giving of blood by

Mother has seriously put her own health into jeopardy, and my brother Ted's, because she is still nursing him. I have lost several pints of blood and need more, but no more is available because of cost. Our family just did not have any money.

Awake in the County Hospital bed after many days, the daily diet is cream of tomato soup; cream of every kind of vegetable imaginable is fed to me for many weeks. How I dislike cream of tomato soup or any kind of creamed vegetable soup! This is the time I really became sick of anything that has a milky taste. Ice cream is one item I love, because it has no milky flavor, and it is cold, sweet, and soothing. I can smell cream of tomato soup from afar, and I must remove myself from the area before I get sick.

Other than the cream soup, things I dislike are anything with coconut because it tastes like soap, and then there is the old health medicine that Mother feeds us by a large tablespoon daily, and that is cod liver oil. After swallowing cod liver oil, Mother gives us a small wedge of orange, which chases the terrible flavor away. If everyone in United States is swallowing that awful- tasting thing, the cod fishermen should be making a lot of money during these Depression times. I know that many Italian families eat salt-dried codfish they call *bacalao* that they must soak overnight to get the salt out and soften the meat. At least *bacalao* has no cod liver oil flavor because they must have put it all in the bottle of medicine.

The nurse wheels me to the solarium where I can warm up in the sun and get the much-needed vitamin D. The solarium is a glass-overhead room that is built to capture the maximum sunlight during the day. It is also built in such a way to protect the patients from wind and rain. I spend hours in the solarium just dozing away, hoping that I can leave and play with my friends.

We ask Father for donuts, but he says that those children who are now eating them will die from eating too many donuts. The sugar and fat are bad for us, especially when we are children. Our family does not eat sugar or fat. The two children who eat donuts every day on the front doorsteps of their home is Japanese- American but they look different. Their heads are large and rounder, fingers are chubbier, even though they are obese, eyes are different, and body is rounder. When we make fun of them, Father tells us not to talk bad about anyone, because it is not nice, and they can't help the way they look. The children did die early in life and they both suffered from Down syndrome. We did not even ask for donuts or candy from that day on.

Walking To School
U. S. Grant Grammar School

My grammar school is U. S. Grant, located some seven short blocks away from my home, on Empire Street. Our neighbors are a couple with a teenage son, and next is an Italian family with many girls. One is married and lives across the street. The last is a group of small houses which are actually shanties, with Dust Bowl families living there. Housing is difficult to find because of the influx of people from the Dust Bowl states and immigrants from other countries. People are living in shacks that are substandard housing. A tall person must bend over to get into the shanty. It does look cozy and neat inside. At least these families have shelter, unlike the hobos with bedrolls who ride the rails which run behind their shacks.

The walk to school is around the corner at the railway crossing, where a signalman steps out onto the middle of the street and stops all traffic with his sign during the daylight hours, or a lantern at night, when a train passes through clanging the bell, blowing its moaning, loud steam whistle, and quite often spewing huge black smoke from its smokestack. There is no traffic on this corner of Sixth and Empire streets, but several blocks either way is where there is far more traffic and no signalman there. Instead, there is an electric signal and bars coming down to stop traffic.

The steam engine train passes on, pulling many boxes, refrigerated, and flat cars, and eventually the caboose follows at the end with a train employee hanging on with a signal flag or a lantern in his hand, ready to give communication to the engineer up front. The freight train passes on with a *"clickity-clack, clickity-clack"* rhythm of the wheels on the rail. The chug-chug of the engine and the ding-ding of the bell have long passed, as well as the blast from the whistle. All this, when it happens late into the night or early morning, wakes me up, because the house does shake as the huge train rolls on by. The people living in the shanties must be rattled when the train passes, because they live closer to the railroad tracks than our family.

During the famous 1849 Gold Rush of California, many people came from the eastern United States to make it rich themselves but found that mining for gold is slim pickings so many of these people starts to farm because the soil is so fertile. Fresh vegetables were in high demand. demand. Other immigrants from countries including China and Japan found that either farming or service-related business is more profitable than panning or digging for gold. These service-related businesses included buying and selling vegetables, as well as shipping them to other cities.

Trains made it possible for farmers to ship their produce and fruits rapidly to the large cities in California and to other states. All this started in the late 1800s, when rail became our main mode of rapid transportation for people and goods. Rome became at great empire over two thousand years ago because they made cobblestone roads leading to Rome, thus making it easier for their soldiers to travel by foot from place to place, and supplies moved rapidly with them. The United States became a great nation because the railroads made it possible for people to travel rapidly and all kinds of goods to be transported quickly and economically.

Chinese coolies or laborers working the rails made this all possible in the western United States. When the railroad was completed, these same workers were without a job, a job, drifting to drifting to Chinatowns located throughout the large cities in the West. They, like the Japanese laborers, lived in boarding houses until work became available to them.

Next to the railway track is a large packing shed with a loading dock that runs the length of the packing shed, which is about one hundred yards long. The railroad spur to this shed is filled with refrigerated cars that will be loaded with crates of vegetables, then iced for their long-distance ride. Often, this shed is operating night and day during the harvest times and shipping vegetables and fruits throughout California and other states, including northeastern states and Canada.

Crates of fruits and vegetables have labels that are very colorful. The smaller crates, which hold about twenty-five pounds of goods, are called L.A. lugs. Some members of the Dust Bowl families living in the shacks alongside the tracks at the corner work in the packinghouse. The work is seasonal, but any job is welcomed during these hard times in the United States. Pickle processing plants are located one block north on Jackson Street. Finally, after a block of residential homes, is my grammar school.

Class is not interesting at school, because I have a difficult time understanding the teacher, who is speaking English. She has a difficult time understanding my English, because it is heavily accented and mixed with Japanese. They say I'm speaking Pigeon English. Can pigeons talk, like parrots?

Chinatown San Jose
Chow mein Family dinner

Father takes the family to the Chinese restaurant one block away to the north. We, including Granduncle Nobujiro, walk the short distance. It is a happy occasion for all of us because we are eating at a restaurant. Not everyone can have a family meal at a restaurant during these hard Depression days.

Father orders a very large plate of chow mein with strips of barbecue pork on top. It must be a very large plate to feed three adults and six children. I pour soy sauce over my plate of chow mein and add some hot mustard for flavor. There is nothing like hot mustard on chow mein because it becomes spicy. The meal is filling, and we are all satisfied. For my parents and uncle, it is doubly satisfying, because it beats cooking and washing dishes. Father speaks Chinese to the people in the restaurant. He learned how to speak Chinese during the early 1920s, when he spent two years in China.

He speaks Spanish to the Filipino and Mexican field hands on the farm, he speaks Italian to Old Man Sacamano, and now he is speaking Chinese to the restaurant people. German is also spoken to people who understand it. Father did spend four years in Berlin during the early 1920s, prior to his moving to the United States via Mexico to live near his parents in Los Angeles, a steppingstone. Why doesn't he speak to us in English at home instead of Japanese?

We live in a neighborhood where Japanese is spoken freely, and with his limited English, he can still be understood at work. I hope I can speak all those languages when I get older, but first I must learn English, not pidgin English.

Across the street from the Chinese restaurant are rows and rows of wooden shops fronting the brick row apartments or flats, with hundreds if not thousands of Chinese occupants. This is Chinatown, and around the corner is Japanese Town, sometimes called Japan town. Everyone looks alike, and even I cannot tell one from the other if I did not know them. Some Chinese do wear their traditional clothes, however the Japanese wear Western clothes, because the silk kimonos are expensive and too noticeable. The Western clothes are not the country-and-western style, with a cowboy hat and boots. The Japanese who immigrated to the United States are here to stay and willing to change their lifestyle, including the clothes they wear. I find it very difficult wearing *getah*, a wooden shoe.

At the corner of Sixth and Taylor is an old brick. building so small that it can only hold a dozen or so adults inside. This is an *On Leong* or *Tong* building, as some people say, but it is a religious temple for the Chinese. I go inside by stepping over the doorway into a dark temple, then around a thin wall in front of the door. This stepping over an obstacle and around another obstacle is to keep the devil out. Devils cannot go through these obstacles because they travel in a direct line. It looks abandoned because there no structures near this small red brick building. When there were thousands of Chinese living in this area, this temple flourished, and many incense were lighted and prayers were said.

Tolerance is great here in this neighborhood, even right now when Japan is running rampant through China and other countries of Asia, but here we do business with each other as usual. Japan already took Manchuria *(Manchuko)* and Korea *(Chosen)* through forced military action. That's a nice way to say war.

War is not nice; people—especially children like me—die needlessly. Children are starving in every war, and many are abandoned, lost, or orphaned. These children are destined to perish. Abandoned babies crawling on dirt roads seeking refuge is not a pretty sight, and it does happen. It is terrible to be abandoned, lost, or orphaned when you cannot fend for yourself, so young, needing protection from a mother or an adult. Older children are used as soldiers. They have not experienced childhood, and now they are carrying weapons or supplies for the army.

What are the rich and powerful people thinking about when they cause these wars? Riches and power are not worth it when human lives are at stake. People have been known to rebel against their own powerful country that is suppressing them. The United States is one of the countries that was formed through rebellion, and it will not be the last country to do so. Children who were soldiers and survived into adulthood are the ones who will be the ones either leading rebellions or fighting for their beliefs. Horrible experiences of war will never be forgotten, not even by children.

First Christmas In Camp
Candy, nuts, and gifts

Since we first arrived at this concentration camp called Heart Mountain Relocation Center in the state of Wyoming, snow has been on the ground, drifting in patches all along the way to school and everyplace else. This is the first time many of us Japanese Americans have seen snow, much less experienced the bitter cold of the high altitude near Yellowstone Park. Even the wool cap, earmuffs, extra layer of warm clothing, and muffler don't keep the icy chill from the body.

The elementary school is a short distance from our barracks, just below our lower block. It doesn't take long to get there when you run in the wintry cold to the warm school room. A volunteer fourth-grade teacher has already stoked the embers and placed more coal into our potbellied stove to warm the classroom.

Teacher has everything ready for us; that is, the blackboard has been cleaned and new instructions printed carefully in large enough block letters for the person sitting furthest away to be able to read it. Many hardwood desks that are bolted to a cast-iron frame are all facing the teacher's desk and the blackboard. Desktops have a groove for pens and pencils, with a hole on the upper-right corner for the inkwell. The inkwell is full, and the pen lays next to the sharpened pencil, because the day prior, we all had to prepare this for the new day, including erasing the blackboard and cleaning the erasers by striking them together outdoors to rid them of the chalk dust. There are more than twenty of us in the class, and everyone gets a chance to take part in cleaning the classroom, blackboard, and erasers. Isn't that nice?

The teacher teaches us not only to read and write, but to express ourselves orally. Arithmetic is also taught, along with history and geography. This is where I first came across the subject of ancient cliff dwellings of the Southwest in the United States. I made a promise right then and there that I will visit Montezuma's Castle, a cliff dwelling, in Arizona. We also learned about the Volga Boatmen pulling their crafts laden with goods by a long rope up the Volga River in Russia, singing a song. I have no desire to be a boatman.

This class is much more interesting than U.S. Grant Grammar School in San Jose. She even teaches us to write a fiction story all of our own thoughts. Now, this is interesting, and what thoughts and ideas we have at such a young life with such imaginations! Well, I wrote one with a title and a fictitious name that was so inappropriate that it cannot be mentioned here. Everyone laughs and the teacher turns beet red. Naturally, I was so embarrassed that from that day on I've had writer's block.

My two sisters, who are twins, have a young Quaker for their teacher. My young teacher is very tolerant and does not try to correct my strong accent but does correct the improper English usage. According to my sisters, their teacher is also tolerant and wants us all to have the best education in the elementary school. I have not seen or experienced any disciplinary action for infraction of school rules. We Japanese Americans obey the teachers, unlike the grammar school in San Jose, where we were disciplined for unknown reasons, like English usage.

Our young volunteers teach us with love, unlike the strict discipline of older teachers.

Halloween is soon approaching, and the teacher has everyone cut pumpkins, spiders, witches' hats, etc. from colored construction paper to pin and paste around the classroom. The reason for this celebration is given by the teacher, but it quickly goes over my head. Everything is new to me, even though the grammar school in San Jose did have these days, which to me is not important or interesting. Japanese American culture is completely different than the American culture, and our teacher is teaching all of us to assimilate us into Americans, even though Heart Mountain is full of Japanese.

Thanksgiving holiday decorations are cut and hung throughout the classroom. This a very colorful season indoors, while the scenery outside is white of the snow and the strong contrast black of the tar-paper barracks. The first Thanksgiving Day by the Pilgrims and American Indians is explained to us, and how sharing and giving thanks for a bountiful crop is important.

Colorful wild turkeys are made from construction paper and pasted together. Some students love to eat white paste, but I find that it has a very bland flavor. Maybe salt and pepper may help enhance the flavor. Did you know that maple leaves come in a wide variety of colors? We cut out maple leaf shapes from all the different colors of the construction paper.

Thanksgiving Day meal at the mess hall is not celebrated with decorations and a fancy dinner table set. We get in line with our stainless-steel mess tray and are served our regular food. Japanese culture is quite different than the Americans at this time of the Second World War. Americans celebrate Thanksgiving with a very large dinner like the Japanese celebrate New Year's. New Year's celebration lasts for three days of feasting. This New Year's will be different indeed.

There are very few Christians here in camp, and all the teachers are Christians who encourage us to brighten the classroom with the holiday spirit decorations. The teacher teaches us to cut out snowflakes and Christmas tree shapes from colored construction paper. These are strung on a line, pasted to windows, and even tacked onto the wood walls. Christmas cards are made using pen and ink and even crayons.

Christmas carols are taught, and we all sing with the guidance of the teacher. I have been singing these carols for several years in Sunday school in San Jose, California. My sisters and I have no trouble in singing, often leading the rest of the children. Many of my friends have never sung Christmas songs, because they are Buddhists. These friends of ours must memorize each song, as I have long ago. We sing "Hark, the Herald Angels Sing," "We Three Kings," "Silent Night," and "Joy to the World," among the many other songs that make up this happy occasion.

Mother sings along with us at home, although she is a Buddhist. Despite being almost totally deaf, Mother really is into music of all sorts, and does not let her impairment bother her. Her most favorite religious song is "Amazing Grace." This pre-Christmastime is sad in a way because we are in a camp, treated as prisoners. The music does bring out the cheerfulness of the season.

Many elders in the camp, as well as the young adults, feel that the Christmas decorations and singing the carols is teaching us children a new religion that they have not given permission for. The older people are complaining that the Japanese culture is being eroded by this teaching. They cannot do much, because they are under the control of the United States government and the United States Army who are guarding us. We are in a concentration camp, and orders are orders, even from the young volunteer female teachers. These teachers are doing their job, and they are teaching the three R's, Reading, 'Riting, and 'Rithmetic. A little Religion is in with it during the Christmas season. The elders often say, "Gaman suru hazu." In another words, "You have to tolerate it." The other saying is "Shikata ga nai." This is "cannot be helped."

As if I didn't know the story of Jesus's birth, our teacher explains the story especially the birthplace in a small village called Bethlehem. This is another place that I would like to visit. It would be perfect to visit Nazareth, the Sea of Galilee, and Jerusalem. Our teacher makes us feel that such places still exist and must be visited, which I will do eventually.

Mother does not send us to Sunday school. The Christian church is no longer assisting us with food and clothing. I do miss Sunday school but enjoy playing with my newfound friends on Sundays.

Elders feel that the family values are being undermined, because the children are not eating with their families, but instead eating with their classmates and friends of their age. The children are being taught religion and not philosophy of life as Buddhists. In fact, children are no longer saying Grace or *"ita dake masu"* at the beginning, nor *"gotso sama"* at the end of each meal. They no longer care; they just rush into the mess hall and eat rapidly just to get out into the snow to play games. The war has changed everyone, especially the children.

Since many of us have never played in the snow, Mother has to teach us how to roll a ball of snow into a large ball and make a snowman. While we make the snowman, Mother would throw snowballs at us, and then we all get full of snow and have a lot of fun. Do you know how difficult it is to throw a snowball at your mother, whom you love so much? It is a good thing that the snow is soft. Later, we build a wall, which protects us, and then we have a real snowball battle. This battle is a lot of fun, until we learn to harden the balls by wetting them down with water and freezing them overnight outside in the cold. These "snow" balls really hurt. New rules of snowball fights are set.

Mother buys figure skates through a mail-order book and she teaches us how to ice skate at the rink next to the high school. This ice-skating rink is a large football field that has a low levee around it and water added onto the field. The cold of the Wyoming air freezes the water. It is fun skating the figure eight forwards and backwards. Races are on, and competition runs high, but it is all sportsmanship without bitter feelings. "Crack the whip" is fun, but when I become the last person on the chain, the speed is terrific, and "crack," I go flying on the ice when I can't hold on any longer, eventually falling to skid and stop. It is really painless, maybe because of all the clothing that acts like padding, or my body is so cold that I cannot feel the fall.

Mother's feet are small, but still, we must add paper in the toe of the skates for a better fit. Although born in Northern California by Sacramento, she was raised by her Russian grandmother in the mountains of Hiroshima, Japan until she turned sixteen and returned to California. Her grandmother taught her how to skate. Mother is so beautiful, just gliding on the ice, smiling with her rosy cheeks, and having more fun than us children. It is wonderful to see her so happy, reliving her childhood. I bet that Great-grandmother and Mother had many wonderful moments ice skating together.

Fortunate families here who have sons in the U.S. Army often receive extra packages of goodies. The sons who volunteered for military service know their families in the camp have just the bare necessities and very few luxuries. Government officials screen even the packages and Christmas gifts. I wonder how many items these officials steal, if any. However, most candies, canned goods, and cigarettes get through.

On Christmas Eve, our very first in the concentration camp, people gather at the high school gymnasium to receive a brightly colored package for Christmas. Every child is given at least a bag of hard rock Christmas candy, a bag of nuts, and a gift. We now have toys, games, dolls for the girls, puzzles to share, and even crystal radio kits. Well, dolls are out for me, but my sisters just love them. When the storm comes and everyone has to be indoors, except to go to school or to eat, we have these new toys and games to keep us occupied. For many of us children, this is the first Christmas gift, greatly appreciated in our family of seven young children.

All our life, Father has forbidden us to have candies of any kind, because they are bad for the teeth, and eating too much of it will kill us, like the two overweight young girls in San Jose. However, this Christmas, he has allowed us all to have the sweet, delicious hard rock Christmas candy. The flavor is outstanding, and the taste just lingers in the mouth so cool, especially the striped mint ones. It didn't take too long to finish my bag. I wonder why my sisters did not want to share their candy with me. This is truly the best Christmas that we have had, and the candy is a taste to die for, because it is like I went to heaven.

Each gift is labeled with the address of the person who donated it from all over the United States. Many are from Christian organizations. American people have rallied at Christmas for the children in the concentration camps, for fellow Americans.

Activities In The Camp
Growing Up

On clear nights, I can see millions upon millions of bright stars that make up the Milky Way and the universe, with occasional shooting stars streaking by silently to wake me from this dreamlike state. The barbed-wire fence may keep me from enjoying freedom, but it cannot fence in my mind from roaming the starfilled universe for the utmost freedom of all with God. It is one mile high here at Heart Mountain, and that much closer to heaven than in San Jose, even though we are in a concentration camp.

When storms come roaring to this camp, huge hail drops suddenly and covers the ground, until the dark brown soil becomes white with ice. Snowstorms rage and blow drifts of white mass onto the sides of buildings and barracks, bringing the biting cold with it. Late-summer rains drench the ground, making the trip to the restroom and mess hall extremely soggy and messy. When my nose is not running, I can smell the air and wet earth.

The most eerie sensation that I have ever experienced is when three twisters off in the dark northeastern sky were moving slowly side by side toward the southeastern sky. They are awesome and spectacular, drawing everything in their path into the dark sky above them. Luckily, these twisters were miles away and did not affect this camp. Can you imagine hundreds of barracks being drawn up into the funnel and up and away into the dark clouds above?

For children, a simple box becomes a train, ship, car, tank, castle, fort, or anything the mind wants. It becomes a secure container for baseball, basketball, and any other sports gear or toys. Many shoeshine boxes and useful pieces of furniture are made from a simple crate.

Outside, children dig. A trench is dug with tunnels. Trench warfare inside a concentration camp? Yes, we have trench warfare. Inside a tunnel room, war plans are made, and war begins. Outside in the trench, we use wooden sticks for rifles, and yell bang, bang, and duck before getting shot at. It takes real team effort to dig all the trenches and tunnels.

Later, it takes real team effort to fill the holes and level everything to keep the adults happy. We know how to try the patience of mothers and fathers. Mothers are now happy because the clothes are cleaner and the hair free from dirt. Crawling in the dirt weakens the knee area of trousers and toes of our leather shoes. Holes have to be patched. Even our socks have to be damed so we can get extra wear out of them. After all, we are expert children. Every child must be unleashed and allowed to play with other children until exhausted, and our family's love helps us to do this. We do have this freedom in the camp without the soldiers bothering us, and only our parents can stop us.

There are games to be played or friends to be made. In our version of tag, one member of the team throws a ball over the roof of the barracks. An opposing team member catches the ball, runs around the barracks, and tags another on the opposite side. The object is to capture the opposing team and make them part of your team. Children from other

barracks and blocks all come to participate, making new friends. Games such as tag, hide-and-go-seek, and kick-the- can go on until after the sun has set and we cannot see by the light of the moon. Hiding territory can be anywhere in the block, except in the barracks, restrooms, or mess halls. Games are really enjoyable exercise, and we have plenty of energy to expend.

Children will play games at every opportunity, indoors, outdoors, in the sun, in the rain, and even in the snow. We are so full of energy that keeping us occupied and getting us completely tired is the only way we can be tolerated. The happy children yell and laugh, enjoying the camp life. Is this any different than at home in San Jose? I have more friends here in camp than when I lived in San Jose. More of them are my same age group.

Board games such as Monopoly, checkers and "Goh" are played at night or when inclement weather outdoors keeps us indoors during the day. "Goh" is a game played with small, flat, oval white and black chips placed on the grid of a board. The object is to line up five ("goh" means five in Japanese) chips in a straight line. In the meantime, one tries to stop the other person from lining up five chips. On the same "Goh" board, war can be played. The object is to try to encircle your opponent with chips. The winner is the person who can encircle one or several chips. Adults play games on the "Goh" board day and night. Is this because time has no meaning to a person incarcerated for an unknown length of time for just being a Japanese American?

Monopoly 1s one game that can take hours upon Montgomery Ward and Sears and Roebuck.

There are schools all the way to a high school. Mother belongs to a sewing class with many women attending. There is even a newspaper called The Sentinel to give us news of the camp and happenings of the outside world. The camp is a city in itself, with a jail, I should mention. Movies are shown in the next block up from us toward Heart Mountain, and I enjoy the Japanese samurai movies we are allowed to see. My favorite seating area is in front of the first-row benches, where all the children lie down, looking up at the screen.

People are allowed to leave to work in other states because laborers are scarce. Much leave for the sugar beet fields in Idaho and Utah. No one is allowed to return to the coastal states. Some do learn to sort baby chicks and separate them as eventual hens or fryers, etc., and then seek work at large poultry farms. These chicken-farm workers also check eggs for fertility status. Do they really send the unfertilized eggs to our mess hall so more egg foo yung can be made?

The cooks get up early in the morning to have all the breakfast ready when the sun comes up, and the scullery people clean and wash the mess gear, the kitchen, and the eating area. These mess hall workers love to scrub the floors every day with soap and water. The complainers go back to their rooms and complain some more while warming themselves by the potbellied stove about not being able to farm like they used to, while the rest of the nation is suffering from a coal and fuel shortage. Did they forget that farming is a hard life with lots of physical labor from sunup to sundown, and not making money at it, and often marbles indoors and outdoors. I have a steelie shooter and consider myself a good shooter, but then, so does everyone else. The agate, aggies, I shoot at and knock out of the circle are mine to keep. One has to be very careful shooting at aggies too close with a steelie, because the force at close range will crack the fragile aggies. Marbles is not a game Mother likes. Boots wear out, and Mother has to order a new pair from the catalog. No one owns two pairs of dress shoes in camp except the wealthy.

Near the main gate, by the motor pool and shops, a large hole is dug, and water added. The hardpan retains the water and what water is lost is through evaporation or us kids drinking it. This is our swimming hole, and we drink a lot of water here. We sure need this swimming hole, because it is hot during the summer on the Wyoming plains. Mother teaches me how to dog paddle first, while staying by the edge of the pool where it is not deep. Later, she advances me to swimming the sidestroke, then on to the backstroke, as well as the crawl. This is very important to me, because I am a skinny kid and very sick for a long time after the tonsil operation. This is building me up, not only in physical being but also in being a good swimmer among the other boys of my age. I was never afraid of swimming across the pool or staying under water, swimming a distance. My prestige has grown now in just one year in camp. I can ice skate and swim, all because Mother taught me. Not all the boys can do this at first because they don't have my mother.

I don't know how to play baseball or basketball, and I'm not very good at it because I cannot judge the speed of the ball coming at me. Our playing field has lots of stones to make it difficult to run and play on.

Usually, I'm the last to be chosen on a team. There are games or sports called shuttlecock, tetherball, and Ping-Pong that can be played by both boys and girls. Hopscotch is a girls' game, so boys do not play it.

Mother enters me in an after-school music class. Although she is totally deaf in her left ear, and hard of hearing in her right ear, she loves music of all sorts and has the children learn music. Harmonica is her forte, and she buys one through the mail order. She stresses the importance of the proper number of holes the mouth organ must have. I begin to play the harmonica, and also under the guidance of a maestro, play the piano. He has me practice the scales up and down, even sideways, if that is possible. The instructor teaches the old Japanese method of strict rote; he stands at attention behind me with his baton, ready to correct any errors that I make. This is nerve-wracking knowing that the baton will come down on my knuckles if a note or a beat is missed. I've had it with his military type of rote piano lessons, which he punishes with that stinging piece of stick called a baton, which he treats like a military swagger stick. I finally convince Mother that piano lessons are not for me, after she sees the back of my hands.

Even the martial arts class called judo didn't go well with me. After weeks of being thrown by other classmates without me being able to throw them, I quit. The sensei, teacher, keeps telling us that before we can learn this art, we must learn how to fall, and I did fall hundreds of time. It hurts to fall, even when you know how to break your fall and roll.

Kendo is fencing, Japanese style. The warriors of old in Japan practiced kendo to keep in shape and perfect their skill in swordsmanship. The kendo weapon is made of split bamboo, tied at sections, and formed into a sword. The fighters wear padded clothing, an armor in a sense, to lessen the bone crushing blow from the kendo stick. A mask which looks like a baseball catcher's mask is worn, and the top of the skull area is padded well. I don't care how well it is padded; it didn't protect me from being knocked out by the killer kendo stroke coming down on me full force. I quit. In fact, I became a quitter in all the after-school classes Mother had me enroll in. Anyway, warriors nowadays use a rifle. I often wondered why they didn't have a class in archery. Maybe using the guard on the tower as a target is too tempting.

Boy Scouts of America in Heart Mountain, Wyoming Troop 31 is the group I belong to, and Mother buys the uniform and neckerchief. Troop 31 was the Japanese American Boy Scout troop from the Boy le Heights area of Los Angeles, California, as I understand. This is where they teach us how to be a good scout and learn a little about camping and survival. We are in a camp, and they are teaching us kids about camping and making a campfire.

Since there are about 10,000 of us in this camp, there are many functions similar to any city of this size. Cody and Powell are cities near our camp, and the total population for both does not reach 10,000. We have doctors, dentists, and even nurses to take care of our health needs. There is a small canteen in our block that sells the most basic items for us, like Bull Durham and Prince Albert pipe tobacco. It is not a department store. Also on our block is a post office where mail is picked up and orders can be made through the catalogs like Montgomery Ward and Sears and Roebuck.

There are schools all the way to a high school. Mother belongs to a sewing class with many women attending. There is even a newspaper called The Sentinel to give us news of the camp and happenings of the outside world. The camp is a city in itself, with a jail, I should mention.

Movies are shown in the next block up from us toward Heart Mountain, and I enjoy the Japanese samurai movies we are allowed to see. My favorite seating area is in front of the first-row benches, where all the children lie down, looking up at the screen.

People are allowed to leave to work in other states, because laborers are scarce. Many leave for the sugar beet fields in Idaho and Utah. No one is allowed to return to the coastal states. Some do learn to sort baby chicks and separate them as eventual hens or fryers, etc., and then seek work at large poultry farms. These chicken-farm workers also check eggs for fertility status. Do they really send the unfertilized eggs to our mess hall so more egg foo yung can be made?

The cooks get up early in the morning to have all the breakfast ready when the sun comes up, and the scullery people clean and wash the mess gear, the kitchen, and the eating area. These mess hall workers love to scrub the floors every day with soap and water. The complainers go back to their rooms and complain some more while warming themselves by the potbellied stove about not being able to farm like they used to, while the rest of the nation is suffering from a coal and fuel shortage. Did they forget that farming is a hard life with lots of physical labor from sunup to sundown, and not making money at it, and often starving? They never had it so good, as my parents would say.

Being in this camp gives my parents some time to recuperate from the hardship of life during the Depression years of trying to raise seven pre-adolescent children and take care of an old uncle. They do not have to worry about where the next meal comes from, much less preparing it for the children while here in this camp. The barracks gives shelter and some warmth from the aid of the small potbellied stove. This is a great life for them, although we are living with the bare necessities of life. Father earns a little money working in the camp with the rest of the men and women, and each member of our family is given a small allowance for clothing and toilet articles.

Father makes several getahs, wooden shoes like slippers, so we can walk to the restroom without soiling our regular shoes or boots. These also save wear and tear on shoes which cost money and must be ordered through the catalog from either Montgomery Ward or Sears and Roebuck. The getahs are made from two-byfours and other wooden slats nailed together, and a thin rope as straps to hold our feet onto the getahs, similar to the Japanese straw slippers which some call flipflops. The getahs have two wooden strips over one inch thick, nailed to the wooden slat, thus elevating the feet nearly two inches above the surface of the ground, which is often muddy or snow-covered. It does keep the feet dry and clean most of the time. Shoes and getahs are not allowed in the bedroom area, and they are removed and set in the hallway mud room to air and dry. This makes the bedroom cleaner, without the dirt and mud being tracked into the room, which means less work for my sisters while sweeping the floor. Pop did nail a metal shoe scraper to the end of our porch steps, so the shoes are not tracking in so much dirt into the hallway.

Since leaving Santa Anita Assembly Center, I have not seen anyone doing their early-morning stretch exercises. It is so cold here in the winter that the early morning stretching is usually done in the barracks room, close to the potbellied stove. As far as I'm concerned, there are more important things to do so early in the cold morning. The stove must be stoked, and fresh coal added, as well as emptying the ash into the ash bin by the boiler room. Then the stainless-steel pail that brought ash to the bin must be filled with coal by the boiler room and carried to the barracks for our stove.

The morning ritual of brushing my teeth with either liquid or powdered teeth cleaner, washing my face, applying a greasy rose-scented pomade to my hair, and combing it down, etc. must be taken care of prior to having a morning breakfast. Hot showers are not taken early in the morning, but rather at night, just prior to going to bed. The hot shower warms the body enough to where one could get between the cold sheets and keep warm until sleep comes. Going to school after breakfast is our next agenda, so all in all, morning stretch exercise has long been forgotten. Mother teaches us how to warm the insides of our clothing then wear them prior to going out into the bitter cold outdoors.

Mother tells us about her Russian grandmother who use to send her to school holding a warm sweet potato (sato imo). This keeps her hands warm and later it can be eaten. Sweet potatoes are eaten instead of rice because rice fetches a better price than sato imo.

Sam's Place
Drinking and Gambling in Camp

Possession of alcohol is illegal in all concentration camps. The canteen will not sell it, nor will the government allow the sale to the internees. I guess the government is afraid that the people will not use good judgment when drunk, and cause disturbances in the camp that may become a national embarrassment.

Father is not a person who sits around and does absolutely nothing about this ruling. After all, Sam Saito is an old-fashioned Japanese man with strong traditional feelings, which include drinking sake-a Japanese rice wine-for festive, religious, or other occasions, including warming the body during the bitter cold Wyoming winter season. This drink also makes a person forget that they are in a concentration camp. In fact, there are many reasons, according to Father, to have a cheer or two or three at any time. He is thinking!

Father goes to several mess halls and gets rice here, raisins there, several Crock Pots from God knows where, sugar, gallon jugs, and a starter called koji. Koji is fermented rice or rice mold that the government furnishes us in camp, maybe because it is part of the Japanese food staple. This koji is also the main ingredient in making sake.

Father makes sake from rice, sugar, and koji. He also makes wine from raisins.

After fermenting in Crock Pots for some time, the rice wine are globs of white goo and the whole mess of mash is bubbling. The smell is not very appetizing, nor the sight appealing. My parents scoop the goo into their mugs and drink it with gusto. They love this concoction. How can a twenty-nine-year-old mother of seven children born in California love and drink that smelly, white, mushy-looking goo?

The sake is ready, and it is time to transfer the liquid into gallon jugs. The mash and all is put into a flour sack and the end tied very tightly. A large rock is placed on top; the liquid oozes through the sack filtered, then the sake is poured into the gallon jugs and capped.

Everyone who had an active hand in furnishing the ingredients for the sake is given a portion of the liquid gold. This illegal rice wine is a real treat in camp. Even a small cup of this Japanese national drink served hot or cold in camp is a dream come true that there is life here in this desolate, boring world where mankind has forgotten us. It's party time tonight, with lots of singing and clapping of hands to make music. Father is a good singer, especially after getting warmed up with sake.

Early in the cold morning, my sisters and I walk from the barracks onto the snow-covered ground to the laundry room toward the restroom. It is bone-chilling cold with the wind tossing the snow around, making the situation colder, and the chill factor is lower yet. We all are in a terrible hurry to get to the restroom; the cold weather does that to the bladder. In the laundry room, a man who passed out from drinking too much home brew is slumped in the deep sink, with ice-cold water running on his head. He is one cold drunk.

After squeezing all the sake out of the mash, Father saves the leftover pulp for pickling purposes. A layer of the mash is put on the bottom of a Crock Pot. A layer of white radishes (daikon) is put on top of the mash and salted liberally. Another layer of mash is put on top of the radishes and salted; layers upon layers of radishes and mash with salt go in until the Crock Pot is full. In another Crock Pot, cucumbers and long eggplants are also pickled. A wooden slat is placed on top of the layers, and a heavy stone presses the pickles and mash. A white cloth covers the crock jars to protect the contents from dust and other things that the odor attracts.

The room smells of a brew house. Several weeks later, the pickles are ready to eat. They taste wonderful, a little salty and alcohol tangy, but very delicious. It is wonderful to eat this with a big bowl of hot, steaming rice, just like the good old days back in San Jose, California. If too much of this is eaten, one can become a little tipsy, I know, but not like that man who passed out in the deep sink. The Crock Pot is again used to make more sake, and a routine cycle is started. Happy days are here to stay.

Family friends love small gifts of pickles, and we have many friends now. These friends quickly learn to communicate with my mother by talking louder than normal into her right ear. One white radish, cucumber, or eggplant goes a long way with hot steamed rice, and friendship becomes well-bonded. A victory garden from our backyard provides all the vegetables for the pickles. Even the green tender leaves of the red radish are salted, and after one day of marinating, it is perfect for pickled greens with a bowl of rice. Everything can be used for food, and nothing is wasted.

The mess hall food is great and filling, but occasionally, Mother likes to have rice and pickles at home to remind us of the real Japanese food we were accustomed to eating during the hard Depression years not so long ago. To help with the war effort, many Americans including us in camps have victory gardens. We have become sod busters again. There are exchanges of vegetables of all kinds for our pickles. Our newfound friends want Mom to make more of the delicious pickles; I wonder why.

Another war effort help that many of us participate in is collecting tinfoil and wrapping them into a ball and turning it into a collection point, so lightweight airplanes can be made from them. Some candies, gum and most cigarette packages have tinfoil to keep the freshness in. You will be surprised at how many smokers throw these wrappers away, but we find them and make a large ball. Even toothpaste tubes are collected for the zinc or whatever metal it contains.

We gather cow chips from outside the camp to use as fertilizer for the victory garden. Not a pleasant chore, but it does allow us to get out of the camp and hunt for these vegetable growth enhancers. The coal pail carries the water for irrigation. All seeds are ordered through catalogs or sent by friends through mail. Everything is at a premium, but everyone is willing to share what little they have with each other. Our family has little of everything, but pickled in rice wine mash radish that has sprung from one simple seed becomes a great asset for us in friendship and assistance of all sorts.

I remember being picked on by the more affluent Japanese boys in San Jose, but now I have become very popular among the boys from Boyle Heights of Los Angeles. These boys think they are the roughest and toughest guys around, but they are not, that is for sure.

Father does not stop here making rice wine; no, he continues making more sake for his friends and himself so he can have the mash to make more pickles. He somehow manages to squeeze more sake just prior to his last gallon jug of wine. Wine is good for this cold weather, but the mash is better for bringing friends around. It seems that the main product is the mash, and the sake is just a byproduct that can be enjoyed by a few of Father's friends.

Somehow, my parents are able to get the leftover pulp of soy, which is very fibrous, from a person who is making tofu from soybeans. Tofu is another prized commodity among the Japanese who are in camp. This pulp is cooked with carrots and other vegetables and becomes a meal for us. Normally, this soy pulp is discarded, but the Saito family knows how to make good use of it. Depression and thriftiness teach one to survive on soy pulp. Again, nothing is wasted, not even the byproduct of tofu.

A dark, hairy, long root called gobo (burdock) is harvested from our garden, and Pop makes a dish of these all sliced up, cooked, and well-peppered to taste. However, first it has to be soaked in water to leach the bitterness out of it. It is spicy but very chewy and tasty and goes well with rice. How my mother and father love to make simple dishes at home so we can taste the old forgotten flavors that used to be with us not so long ago.

It is very easy to get potatoes from the mess hall. Ask and ye shall receive, and receive we do. These potatoes are baked near the hot potbellied stove at night and eaten as a snack. Sometimes the potatoes are cut in half to share, so everyone has a bite to eat. There is a saying that no child should go to sleep hungry, and the Saito kids did not go to sleep hungry, especially in Heart Mountain camp.

Father's room, F which is the last room in the barracks, has been transformed and is now Sam's Place, where men come to play penny-ante poker and have a cup or two of rice wine and bits of pickled radishes. A Japanese cup of wine is actually less than half a shot glass, or a half ounce, not much, but potent, especially when they have not been able to drink it for months on end. To many Americans, this is just a sip, which it really is, but what a good sip it is. It has a little bite to it when served cold. When served hot, it is sweet and mellow, then it sneaks up on you like that man cooling his head in the deep sink.

The room is smoke-filled, some men rolling their own from a small Bull Durham tobacco bag with ZigZag paper or Prince Albert pipe tobacco from a can. There are very few ready-made Camels or Lucky Strikes smoked because of the cost. It is very difficult for me to roll a cigarette with Bull Durham. Some people are saying that the tobacco is made from the cow chips from bulls. I think they are full of bull. There is a rule for us not to light our cigarettes three on a match, because the third one will get shot by the enemy sniper. By the time the third cigarette is lit, a sniper can bead in on you, and one shot is all it takes. Cub Scout leaders did not teach us this, but someone who has war experience passed the word down. There is another rule that says we must hold the cigarette with our thumb and index finger, cupping the cigarette in the palm, so the enemy sniper cannot see the glow of the ash from afar. We were taught to strike our match toward our body, to avoid throwing a spark and starting a fire. One can start a fire on themselves this way too. The last rule is never to smoke because it will stunt your growth and even brown your teeth. All of us kids tried all the rules to the end. I'm still alive, growing, and my teeth are still white.

Children are forbidden in Sam's Place because of the gambling, drinking, and smoking. I often go in to stock up the coal bin. There are two round tables with chairs. Army blankets cover the tables. I wonder where Father got the extra blankets; maybe he traded for rice or raisin wine. The room is always neat and clean, and Father's cot is tidy and partitioned off in the comer by the door. Father's reputation among some is not great because of this room. He does bring some sort of life from the outside into the camp by his actions. There must be other rooms used for gambling within our camp, but none has sake flowing for their customers like Sam's Place. There is no place like Sam's Place.

Since Father's rules are that his games are at penny ante and very low stakes, no one really loses much at his tables. It is a place to socialize by smoking, drinking, telling lies, and gaming only for the bored adults in the concentration camp. Sam's Place continues to bring joy and happiness to the winners and the drinkers, but mixed feelings to the losers and nondrinkers. The police or the soldiers have not come to raid and close down Sam's Place.

The chief of police-we do have a police department in camp-calls Father in to be jailed for having a gambling room. Gambling is forbidden in all federal prisons, and that goes for concentration camps, which they now call relocation centers, a nice name. Father arrives at the porch of the police department's so-called jail and inquiries about his charges. The chief tells Father in front of a large crowd that has gathered, at Father's request, that he must go to jail for running a gambling room. At this point, Father gestures toward the fence and guard tower, and says that we are all in jail, look at the barbed-wire fence and guard tower, so why put more restrictions on him? Everyone laughs and jeers the chief, until he tells everyone to leave, including Father, because the matter is closed. Father thinks that the chief really wanted to get some rice wine, but it was never offered to the chief, not openly that I know of, and the card games go on.

Shoshone River
And the protectors of River

We are allowed to leave the camp and hike to Shoshone River several miles away, or hike toward Heart Mountain to get our body full of ticks. Some people ride the bus into Cody, Wyoming to do some shopping or just to go sightseeing. I have never hiked to Heart Mountain because of the sagebrush, rattlers, and ticks. Mother plans a family picnic to Shoshone River.

Rivers oftentimes are regarded as holy. It brings life from the mountains to furnish nourishment to the fields to make them fertile. People go to the rivers to pay homage. It is called a pilgrimage. Mother is taking us all on a pilgrimage to the Shoshone River. This outing is something Mother needs to do. We need a family picnic, and she needs to see a river again. A river has meaning to Mother because her family name means Plum River.

Mother manages to get some bologna, a loaf of bread, mustard, and an onion from the mess hall. She wraps a gunny sack around a gallon jug and sews the ends to firmly secure it. This jug is filled, and the sack is soaked with water. The breeze passing through the wet, meshlike gunny sack (a burlap bag) cools the jug, and the water becomes cooler. All the older children help Mother in carrying the picnic items, and we start out early after breakfast toward the river, away from the tick-infested Heart Mountain.

After signing out at the guard shack, we follow the barbed-wire fence line to the edge of the camp. Crossing the railroad tracks, we arrive at the main twolane paved road right leading west to Cody and Yellowstone Park, and left leading east to Powell, Wyoming. There is no traffic. The federal government picked a quiet place for a camp.

Continuing on toward the river, we keep the cornfield to our left and a small creek to our right until we reach the Garland Canal, which furnishes irrigation water to the farms in the area and beyond. The water moves swiftly eastward toward Powell. This is freedom, and even the air smells better.

There is a path leading down to the creek. After we all get to the creek, we look into two conduit pipes made of corrugated steel that allow creek water to flow under the Garland Canal to reach the Shoshone River. One has a little water running through it and the righthand-side pipe is dry. The pipe is large enough for us walk slightly bent over to reach daylight on the other end. The distance is not too far. The echoes of the noise of our passing through resounds, making everything very eerie. Reaching the end of the tube, we arrive to a bright sunlit day again, even though there are the two cliffs on both sides of us and the wall of dirt from the creek to the top of the canal.

On the left cliff of the creek side are many swallow nests made of the gray mud from the creek, and on the right side, there is water pouring out from the rocks. Near the small water outfall, a wild rose bush with several small bright red flowers grows, bringing beauty to this rugged rocky scene. Naturally, Mother picks one rose, smells it, and leaves the others for anyone else who wants to enjoy a little color in their drab living quarters back at the camp. We all get an opportunity to stop to smell the rose.

Mother gets a cup full of the water from the cliff and tastes it and then passes the cup for us to drink the refreshing water. This water is so cool and sweet, unlike the camp water full of chemicals. This stop by the small outfall is so relaxing and enjoyable that we all take a deep breath of appreciation. It is heaven on earth away from the camp, just all of us with Mother. She pours out the camp water from the gallon jug and replaces it with the water from the cliff side. The cool water is poured on the gunny sack.

After our short rest, Mother leads us toward the river. I can hear the rushing of the water just ahead. Several bends later from the pipes, we reach our goal, the Shoshone River. I must have seen rivers before in San Jose, California, but this is awesome. Unlike Guadalupe and Coyote creeks that run through San Jose, this is large, and the water is running swiftly. Rivers have spiritual magnetism to draw people to them; however, today we are the only ones to have made the pilgrimage, and the sight is a wonderful experience for me. There are many large rocks, but she finds a nice place to have a picnic near the rushing river.

Mother makes sandwiches for all of us. A bologna sandwich with mustard and onion is delicious eaten out of doors away from the barbed wire fenced in camp. Enjoying our meal and drinking the cool, sweet water from the jug is the highlight of this picnic. This is our first picnic we have had in a long time. Too bad Father had to stay at the barracks to keep his gambling tables going. He is tending to business.

All of us throw stones into the water surface, trying to make them skip many times. There are so many rocks here that we can spend hours skipping stones. Clay is abundant, and I made bowls while my sisters made dolls. Making dolls is not my bag of bones.

There are tall trees with huge nests on the opposite bank, several hundred feet upstream. Upstream from us on our side becomes a sheer cliff with few trees growing along the bank between huge rocks. Downstream on this side of the river is an inlet with a small boathouse. Across the way is a low-lying area where the land gradually slopes into the river and the river wraps itself around this stretch and disappears around another bend. Although some of us know how to swim, Mother for bids us from getting into the water because it is moving too swiftly. We obey her wishes.

All the food is gone and the water down to its last drop, so Mother starts us back, stopping again to fill the water jug with the cool, sweet liquid coming out of the cliff near the wild rose bush, and picks another rose. Mother has us all drink more of the water from the cliff. Walking back to the camp seems shorter than when we started this morning. What fun we had as a family on a picnic by the side of the river. Mother tells us that she lived near a river with her grandmother and enjoyed it very much. This outing must have brought back many fond memories of her youth.

We signed back in on the log at the guard shack and quickly made our way home to the barracks. It will soon be dinnertime and we will be able to hear the chow bell ringing loudly, beckoning us to enjoy the evening meal.

First, we must change clothes and wash our hands and faces with soap and water. I'm so hungry, I can eat a double serving of whatever they have, even egg foo yung.

A group of us talk of going fishing at the river, but no one has any fishing gear. I manage to get a length of string and several safety pins. No one has any hook, sinker, or fishing line. A survivor always has something that could be used for fishing just in case he has to feed himself in the wilderness. This camp has no survivor, so we must come up with something to catch some trout to bring back. Being boy scouts in Troop 31 at camp did help us improvise for our fishing trip.

A bunch of us kids go to the mess hall early in the morning and get some bread, bologna, potatoes, mustard, and onions for the fishing trip. I borrow Mother's water jug and promise to bring back a gallon of the cool water from the cliff. We need some bait, and one of the guys said that trout will not bite on bread, bologna, or onions, but we can go to the farmer nearby and ask for worms on his land. The farmer is very kind and shows us where to dig near his hog pens where the ground is damp, soft, and smelly. He said that the worms here are big and plump, and that the fish will eat them. We get a can full of worms, and off to the river we go. The farmer calls them night crawlers, and we call them earthworms, same thing.

On the way near the creek and next to the canal, we pick some corn that we can cook over a fire. Everyone has his arms full carrying something which we need on the fishing trip to the river. I fill up the jug with the cool, sweet water pouring out of the cliff below the canal. The jug is heavy with all that water, but I'm happy that we are close to the river. Listening to the rushing water around the bend of this creek makes all of us hurry to the river.

After a long hunt for a stone that is the right size and rough enough that I can tie my fishing line, I add my safety pin and a plump worm to my makeshift fishing gear. The fishing line is thrown in and tied at the other end to a large rock. Not everyone has a fishing line, so a few wanders around, enjoying the riverbank. It is an outing of freedom away from the camp. Going fishing without a line or bait is just as fun as holding on to an expensive rod and reel; at least we are fishing.

We all gather dry wood from the nearby riverbank and build a teepee structure for the beginning of a fire, just as the scout masters use it to cut kindling wood that we put at the base of the teepee. One guy lights a stick match, and just as quickly as the match lights, it is extinguished. The second match starts some smoke at the kindling, but it really does not catch. Everyone is giving his expert advice on how to properly start this fire, but even after several more tries and lots of frustrations, we tear the teepee down and gather dry grass. On top of this grass, we place the kindling. Small, dry twigs are poked into the ground, and a teepee is formed. The match is lit and a roaring fire starts with the dry grass burning the kindling and onto the twigs. Our fire finally becomes a roaring success. We know how to start a fire. To heck with rubbing sticks and stuff, because it is hard enough to start a fire with a match.

The bait is changed several times without a bite from any trout, if there are any in this river. I even try to use some of the moss that drifts downstream occasionally as bait, but this proves to be a bad choice. Finally, one of the guys catches a fish, and what an ugly fish it is. It has a big head with large eyes and mouth at the bottom, instead of in front, like the fish I've caught at the Santa Cruz pier. Saltwater fish are better looking; even the ugly bullheads are prettier. The gray, plump fish is gutted and wrapped in clay and tossed in the fire to bake. All the potatoes and corn are wrapped in clay and baked as well. The fish is called a mud sucker, and it look like it does with the mouth on the bottom, sucking mud. The hour is getting late and we decide to eat the potatoes, corn, and fish. The clay has baked hard and is difficult to crack, making it that much more delicious, we hope. Potatoes and corn are delicious even without salt, it is so sweet and tender. I cannot say the same about the ugly fish. Now I know why they call this fish a mud sucker; it has the flavor of mud, but an oily petroleum mud.

The sun will be setting soon, so off we go back to the camp, where we can shower in the hot shower and get this smell of smoke and mud sucker off. I have to get fresh spring water from the cliff side. Everyone is now running full speed to the gate because the sun has just set. The gate guard will get mad at us for being late. At least he is a kind, older Japanese man who always smiles at us. We reach the gate and find that one of us is missing. We run back, yelling his name.

"I'm here, I'm here!" We hear a faint muffled voice. The guy has fallen in a deep hole alongside the path next to the fence. At least the hole was not that deep, so with our help, he was pulled out. "I thought I was buried in that dark hole."

He thought he had died and was buried. We laughed all the way to our barracks.

We return to the river to ride on the rowboat that is housed in the boat house. The opposite side of the river is tempting to get to; the only way to satisfy ourselves is to cross it by rowboat. Four of us climb onto the small boat built for two adults, and two row as hard as possible to cross the river. Changing rowers several times, we finally cross the river a little downstream from where we started. Working the boat upstream until we couldn't go any further because of the cliff and rocks blocking our passage, we tie the boat securely to a rock. If the river was running faster, we wouldn't have gotten across so simply, if at all.

The main reason for crossing the river is to get close enough to hurl stones with our slings at the large white birds nesting on the tall trees. Some time ago, we all got our leather thongs from our boots and tied them to the leather tongues of the boots to make our slings. The boots are now useless because the laces and tongues are gone. The practice area is outside the camp along the fence line where there are plenty of stones. The football field has more stones, but we might break something there with barracks and the high school nearby.

The tall trees are at a distance from where we are, and we just cannot get to them from here. Many tries fail to reach the birds, much less the trees. Our dreams of getting white bird feathers are now gone. It is easier to get back to the boat house on the opposite bank because we are upstream and need to row to the other bank.

We want to get the feathers to make a headdress just like the Indians. The scout masters told us about uses for big bird feathers. They even explained in detail about cutting the quill in such a way to make pens to write with. We have a lot of ink in school, but no quills. Arrows required feathers for fletches, but the scout masters did not give us any hands-on demonstrations how to make arrows, or even how to chip stones to make arrowheads. Since our expedition to get feathers has failed, we are unable to learn how to use these feathers from the scout masters.

It is spring now and the snow has melted, and many months have passed without the pleasure of going fishing. Hiroshi-who is almost old enough to be drafted into the army- and I arrive at the river, but the spring thaw of snow has the river several feet above the usual water line and rushing very fast downstream. The water is brown from the silt carried from upstream. I toss my line into the murky water several yards upriver from Hiroshi. The line gets caught and I step forward to retrieve the line, when I feel emptiness of my footing, and into the raging dark water I go above my head. Downstream just several hundred yards away is a spillway which I can be carried over and perish. Hiroshi sees me disappearing into the water and he reaches over and grabs my hair and saves me from certain death waiting for me downriver.

I arrive back to the barracks still wet from the fall into the river, and quickly get into the hot shower and soap down. There is some calming effect of hot water pouring over my head and heating up my cold body. This is a blessing from God. Thank you, Hiroshi, for being there and alert. It will be some time before thinking about going to the river again. Springtime floods are dangerous, and it is best not to fish during this time. Where do the fish hide during this time of the year?

All the guys agree on getting some of the swallows and keeping them as pets, so boxes are brought with us to the place along the Creekside where they are nesting. The many clay nests will be easy to raid, with the aid of well-aimed stones. This time we don't even think about the Shoshone River just a short walk from here. There are enough baby swallows in the boxes now, so we return to the camp early. Back at the barracks, the sky is dark with hundreds if not thousands of swallows circling overhead. Father finds out that we have the baby chicks and tells us to immediately open the boxes and place them behind the barracks and not to look out the windows. After a while, the birds are all gone, and the boxes empty of the chicks. Father does lay into me with verbal assaults about the chicks being like children and the swallows being like parents protecting them. He has never laid his hand or belt on me. It will be hard for us to go to the river again, because the birds will remember us and maybe attack us while we try to get to the river.

The four of us plan an extra hiking trip to see the spillway dam down the river. I don't have an idea where this spillway is, only that it is several hundred yards from our usual fishing ground. There is no way that we can get there following the riverbank. We just do not want to return to the river via the swallows' nests. After walking by a farm, we reach a wooded area that is a welcome cool spot to rest after a hot hike.

This rest is short-lived because a swarm of yellow jackets attacks us. There are thousands and thousands of stinging yellow jackets coming at me with a vengeance. Well, maybe hundreds, but when you are being attacked, numbers have no meaning, just lots. We run and run to the river and jump in to escape the onslaught. Do you know how cool wet clay feels on yellow jacket stings? It is so soothing that I can almost feel the poison being sucked out of the stings. We managed to get back to the camp without another attack. All dirty and wet we slink back with head hanging low, defeated, and unable to return to the river for fear of the yellow jackets and swallows. We have been beaten by the protectors of the river.

Police
Police interrogation in Camp

Our block has a recreation hall that is used as a Buddhist temple and a religious school on Sundays. Several partitions are placed in front of the altar to form a wall when it is not used for a church. Wooden benches used as pews are moved in front of the partitions and the other three walls, and thus the room becomes a recreation hall. No one bothers the Buddhist temple area, because it is a holy place. The center room of the barracks is a meeting hall for group gatherings, and the room on the other end of the barracks is the post office, where everyone gathers in front for their censored mail during the mail call, to mail personal letters, or to order items from catalogs and buy postal money orders for them.

During the evening, we can go into the temple area and stack benches to form a wall, a barrier, so we have a blow gun fight. The blow gun is a short, lightweight pipe or tubing. A paper dart is placed in the tubing, and with a blast of air from the mouth, the dart is sent off to our target. The paper dart is made from a slick magazine page that is cut into strips about two inches by five inches. The strip is made into a long coneshaped dart by twisting one end of the paper and holding fast to the other. When the cone is the perfect size, the edge is licked to make it stick. The cone is put into the tube and the excess paper is torn off. We try to make many cone-shaped missiles at the barracks, and glue them with airplane glue or paste. Paste is slowdrying, and the cone must be held together for a long time. Airplane glue is faster to dry, but more expensive to buy, and the smell is great, yeah.

The war is fought by blowing the cone missile at the opposing force hiding behind the bench barrier. The object is to run from one barrier to the other on the opposite wall without being hit. The barriers are up against the walls. When we get tired of shooting darts, we get a tennis ball and throw it at each other instead.

The chief of police of the concentration camp call all us kids into his office one at a time and asks if we went into the Buddhist temple area to steal anything. An um is missing, and we are accused of stealing this, because we play there often. Naturally, all of us deny ever going past the walled area and into the temple. We have no need to go into that area, especially when there is no food to eat or toys to play with.

Father is furious that the chief of police for interrogating us without his permission or without him there to see that we are treated properly by the police. He goes to the police station and reads the chief the riot act. Father says that the parents should have been notified, and the parents will question the children if we know the whereabouts of the um. The police must always confide in the parents first, and the parents will handle the situation. We are too young to be led to the station and questioned like an adult criminal. There is bad blood between my father and the chief of police. It is still a wonder that Father has not been arrested for gambling or for having liquor. Could it be that the chief has received some of father's pickled radish or some sake?

Finding out that the um holds the ashes of a dead person in the same room we play in is a shock. If we knew this, we would have left immediately and never come back. In fact, we never did go back to the recreation room. To think that we used to play in that room at night with a dead person's remains there! It still sends shivers up and down my spine, thinking the dead person's remains were in that same room. Will there be another urn full of ashes in that room? It doesn't matter; we won't go back there.

A relative of the owner of the urn notifies the police that it is in her possession. Neither the police chief nor the relative has apologized for the accusation and interrogation of the children.

Toboggan
Sharing the joy of sledding

It isn't possible to sled inside our concentration camp because there isn't a slope steep enough for a sled to slide down. A steep hill is needed to pick up enough speed to have fun. At the northeastern corner of the camp, there is a guard tower set high over the camp, and the road that comes up to it is steep. The camp is completely level, but this section outside the camp overlooks a small arroyo with a road leading up to the tower which is ideal for a long sled run down the road.

A couple of neighbor guys and I plan all summer on how to make a toboggan large enough to carry all of us down that steep hill. After all, we are a team and always do everything together. One small sled is out of the question. The bigger, the better. We will be the king of the sled run with our huge four-man sled.

Wooden barrel staves are not long enough for the toboggan runners, but ideal for skis, but we are not interested in skiing. The metal strapping from the barrel is perfect for the runners' bottom. We will wax the runner for more speed. Carpenters at the camp's shop give us wood and nails. This is a huge, heavy-duty toboggan we are building. We spend days upon days gathering wood, nails, metal straps, and tools. We spend days upon days cutting the wood and nailing the pieces and metal strapping together. It takes real team effort to plan and build this huge thing.

Naturally, there are disagreements on how wide and long the sled will be. Everyone wants to have their ideas implemented in the construction of the toboggan. It is so heavy that it is difficult to move. All this time, we have worked on the toboggan, and we haven't tried to ride it. The enthusiasm is here. The dream of riding down the hill with full force of the icy cold wind with all of us sliding down on this toboggan is here.

The first pre-winter storm leaves several feet of snow, but this is not enough for a toboggan run, so we wait for more snow to be packed down. Snowdrifts cover the back side of my barracks. It is time to haul the toboggan to the hill. We push and pull the heavy toboggan eastward across the slippery high school football field, which has been converted to an ice rink by putting water onto it, and onward toward the steep incline near the guard tower.

Slipping and sliding, we manhandle the toboggan, using all the brute force which we as kids can muster up to move the monster onward. Soon our mittens and scarves are shoved deep into our heavy coat pockets, out of the way. We have no need for them. It is no longer cold for us; we are so hot from all the work. Huffing and puffing, we reached the guard tower.

Other children are sledding with their new bright red sleds, but stare at our huge toboggan with awe. They come down the incline so fast that we know our contraption will come down faster and create a big rooster tail of snow cloud behind us. Disaster! We can't get three feet up the incline. It is too steep for our heavy, long toboggan. Other children are helping us, but our toboggan can't get up the steep hill.

We get a little way up the hill, but the weight of the toboggan slides us down to the bottom, which is only a few feet.

Wait! There is an area that slopes downward from this road several hundred feet away near the firing range where lead rounds are imbedded in the hillside, but all the brass casings are picked up and reloaded for future use by the army. All of us huff and puff, dragging the monster toboggan toward that area where it slopes downhill from the road, a road that circles the camp where guards ride jeeps to their towers. Arriving at the launching area where the white snow slopes, we rest for our second wind and third wind. I'm too tired to count how many times we have stopped to catch our breath getting here.

We push and run with the toboggan and one, two, three, we jump on. We all land on the toboggan with a thud. Crack! Snap! Stop! Our toboggan breaks into two parts. Sadly, we leave our dreams and hard work in the cold, wintry snow. Tonight, the snowstorm will cover the huge sled. The monster sleeps.

Back to the steep guard tower slope we go, where several sleds are shared by many. We carry a new sled that someone let us use up the steep incline on our hands and knees. The effort is not as hard as with our monster of a toboggan we left several hundred feet back and a thousand dreams away. The ride is terrific on this new red sled, and we ride often with the owner. The true joy of every sport is teamwork, trying our best and sharing, regardless of whether we win or not.

There must be a soldier in that guard tower watching us kids screaming as we shoot down the road. It must bring back memories of his childhood. I don't see a soldier in that tower, but then I don't worry about it when there is so much fun in sledding outside the concentration camp.

Pets
Horned toads, prairie dogs, and chipmunks

Horned toads are plentiful and easy to catch here at Heart Mountain. They feed on the millions of red fire ants that live in the camp with us. I keep one home toad in my pocket and take it with me everywhere. Teachers and mess hall cooks don't know it's in my pocket. Mother gets upset with me about the dirty toad, but this toad is not dirty because it is bathed often and is on the ground only to eat. Horned toads are not toads or frogs, they are lizards with horn spines on their head and body. They do not make noise to bother anyone like dogs and cats. There are no dogs or cats in this camp to keep as pets.

My horned toad loves to be let loose near where the red ants are busy looking for food. They now become food for the horned toad. Mother loves green frogs with their mouths open. This is symbol of good luck for her especially the singing green frog she calls Kairu. Loosely translated, it means "to go back home" but also means a frog. Father would call a singing frog "canta rana" in Spanish. The names are all wonderful.

A group of us decided to go exploring by an irrigation ditch that runs near the camp. Below the ditch are prairie dogs looking and barking at us. We ran down and inspect the burrows. There is no way that we can get the prairie dogs out of the holes to make them our pets.

An idea comes, and someone says to run the water from the irrigation ditch above on higher ground into the holes and capture the prairie dogs when they come out. Prairie dogs are not dogs at all; they are rodents of the squirrel family. By these rodents digging in the soil, the land becomes softer so plants can grow. They eat the roots of the plants. Birds of prey and coyotes eat the prairie dogs. All the holes they have dug can cripple cattle, sheep, and horses. To the rancher, prairie dogs are a menace and should be destroyed.

Someone says he will get a couple of gunny sacks made of burlap. We will wait at the holes to capture the prairie dogs if they scramble out of the holes. The sack arrives and the ditch is broken to let water run toward the holes. In goes the water into the holes and outcome the wet prairie dogs into the sacks. They are no longer barking but coughing. Many prairies dogs escape through other holes and scurry off to safety. The ditch is repaired, and the catch is brought back to the camp.

When we get home, Father finds out about the prairie dogs. He reads us the riot act and makes us take them back and release them. We didn't even consider how many of them have drowned because of our action, nor did we consider ruining their burrows where they were protected from the elements and predators. We just don't know anything about life and nature.

I went to get a pet from the creek wall, where there are chipmunks scurrying around. Chipmunks with their striped tails are the cutest pet I have ever seen. They are rodents of the squirrel family, similar to prairie dogs. Several guys already have chipmunks, and I feel left out. The creek wall is full of chipmunks, but when I try to catch one, they all disappear into their holes. I dig at the holes with a branch from a large bush. I dig here and dig there but can't get one chipmunk. The branch snaps in two pieces. I wonder if the chipmunks are laughing at me with their puffy, furry cheeks. Hee hee!

The next day, I went out to the creek, but this time I brought a long, sharp, sturdy stick, and was determined to get a pet. The chipmunks see me and dash for cover. I see several going into one hole, so I dig after them with the sharp stick. Finally, one comes out of the hole, and I reach quickly for it and get bitten. Those buck teeth of the chipmunks are sharp and break my skin. I nursed the bite all the way home.

Mother puts iodine on the broken skin and the iodine hurts more than the chipmunk bite. You know, I may get rabies and start to foam at the mouth and all the kids will run around pointing and yelling, "mad dog! mad dog!" Better yet, I will brush my teeth with toothpaste and run around with the foam around the mouth. I am worried about rabies.

I returned to the creek more determined than ever to capture a chipmunk. Look at the devastation I brought trying to get one cute, striped-tail chipmunk. I could dig for a hundred years and never catch a chipmunk. Along comes a horned toad and I can't resist taking it home. I have a pet again.

<u>Lead Me Home</u>
Where we first began

It's August 1945. Word reaches us that America has bombed Hiroshima with a "genshi bakudan" (atomic bomb) and destroyed the city. Nagasaki was also destroyed later. How can one bomb destroy a city as large as Hiroshima? There is also talk that many military personnel, civilian men, women, and children perished in a flash. Innocent civilians just vaporized into thin air, leaving no bones, nothing. How hideous it must have been in that inferno. Is it true that one bomb can cause such damage that nothing remains? At least 100,000 souls disappeared at Hiroshima. This is the area where my grandparents come from.

Everyone is worried about relatives who live in that area. No country can fight an army that has such a weapon of mass destruction. This is a different kind of war than in the past. The old-fashioned sword-fighting samurais are now dinosaurs. This is the start of an atomic war. What a dreadful time it has become.

The war has ended, and everyone is anxious to go home. But where is home? We as a family have been uprooted suddenly from the old house in San Jose, California. That is not really our home, and now we are being uprooted and returned to San Jose but not to our old residence.

There is packing of the few possessions we have but much more than we had when we first began in 1942. I will miss all the friends I have lived with for the last three and a half years. I will miss the safety of the camp and the three hot meals a day, even the egg foo yung cooked by the master chef. Will the beautiful, clear, starlit night skies here with the Milky Way be the same in San Jose, California? The air is clean and pure here, five thousand feet above sea level. Will San Jose, California still burns the smudge pots, creating thick, black smoke to blanket the valley to keep the vegetable crops and fruits from freezing? The air here is so crisp and clean, unlike the burning tar smell of the smudge filled air of San Jose. This is deep breathing country and San Jose is shallow breathing.

Excitement is in the air as we pile onto the train for our return to San Jose, California, which was once our home. The feeling is different from when we first began loading onto the train in San Jose in March 1942. Then, we did not know where we were going, and the future was very bleak, and sadness and depression could be felt. Will this be our last time to use the family number of 32418? Now we know where we are going, and the future looks very bright, even though we are poor with few more dollars in our pockets and no assets awaiting us at San Jose. There is nothing like starting all over again with nothing but self-determination to succeed. This is going to be a wonderful and exciting life.

Here we go again: one, two, three, etc. Everyone is here except Uncle Nobujiro. Uncle Nobujiro will follow later after housing is found for us. We are excited, even though we have no home, no job, and very few friends, starting over with nothing except determination and hope. The future is bright indeed.

Going home, we cross the tall and majestic, beautiful purple Rocky Mountains. "Lead me home to where we first began" is what we sing in "Amazing Grace." The climb is slow and the engine straining, with thick, black smoke puffing out ahead. We see the engine as we round the bend, and the caboose following behind us, then the engine and caboose disappear. This experience is awesome. The gorge below looks ten thousand miles deep, and the mountain above us reaches all the way to the clouds. There is no end from top to bottom, and we travel across it for hours and hours. The sight is beautiful. Everything is beautiful. America is beautiful. Life is beautiful, because we are all together and homeward bound, caring less of what is ahead and less of what we left behind. This beautiful setting is to be enjoyed right at the present time; the past just left the last turn and the future is coming around the turn and becoming the present time.

Clickety-clack, clickety-clack onto the plains, and we travel alongside the huge endless Great Salt Lake in Utah for hours and hours. It is hot and humid, unlike crossing the Sonora Desert of Arizona in the summer of 1942. The train slows as we pass Reno, Nevada, the gambling, and marriage capital of the United States. There is a sign at the entrance of the town that reads "Biggest Little City in the World." The train picks up speed going downgrade, and we are just hours from San Jose, California. We will pass near Nicolas just a few miles north of Sacramento, California, where Mother was born in 1913.

Upon our arrival at San Jose, an Italian neighbor friend greets us and arranges transportation to the Buddhist temple, a temporary housing and staging area for all who are returning from camp. Hundreds of women and small children purple Rocky Mountains. "Lead me home to where we first began" is what we sing in "Amazing Grace." The climb is slow and the engine straining, with thick, black smoke puffing out ahead. We see the engine as we round the bend, and the caboose following behind us, then the engine and caboose disappear. This experience is awesome. The gorge below looks ten thousand miles deep, and the mountain above us reaches all the way to the clouds. There is no end from top to bottom, and we travel across it for hours and hours. The sight is beautiful. Everything is beautiful. America is beautiful. Life is beautiful, because we are all together and homeward bound, caring less of what is ahead and less of what we left behind. This beautiful setting is to be enjoyed right at the present time; the past just left the last turn and the future is coming around the turn and becoming the present time.

Clickety-clack, clickety-clack onto the plains, and we travel alongside the huge endless Great Salt Lake in Utah for hours and hours. It is hot and humid, unlike crossing the Sonora Desert of Arizona in the summer of 1942. The train slows as we pass Reno, Nevada, the gambling, and marriage capital of the United States. There is a sign at the entrance of the town that reads "Biggest Little City in the World." The train picks up speed going downgrade, and we are just hours from San Jose, California. We will pass near Nicolas just a few miles north of Sacramento, California, where Mother was born in 1913.

Upon our arrival at San Jose, an Italian neighbor friend greets us and arranges transportation to the Buddhist temple, a temporary housing and staging area for all who are returning from camp. Hundreds of women and small children sleep on cots in the gymnasium next to the Buddhist temple, while the men and boys sleep on pews in the basement of the temple. This is the start of our new freedom at home. We are starting at the bottom of the ladder, and now, step by step, we will climb to a much better life.

This is where we first began.

__Housing After Camp__
1945 - 1950 Substandard living spaces

It is difficult sleeping on a hardwood pew for Father and me in the basement of the Buddhist temple, but freedom under this condition is better than being in camp with no bright outlook. Thank goodness our stay after arriving from Heart Mountain Relocation Center, Wyoming is brief at the temple. Mother and my sisters crowd together and sleep on cots close to other women and children in the gymnasium, next to the mess hall several yards from the temple.

There is absolutely no privacy here, and plenty of gossip about the faults of other families. The din of snoring and flatulence must keep many awake. The only privacy is the white sheets hanging in partitions of each family section. At least at this time of everyone's life, showering has become a daily routine for the health and happiness of all. In the concentration camp, hot and cold water were always readily available, which we took full advantage of. This daily habit makes living in close quarters much more bearable and healthier.

My parents do not allow us to talk badly about other people, but we know that they talk about us, especially about Mother's hearing problem and of the many children in our family. So far, we have survived the Depression and the camp during the war. We are a large family, but we have fun because of the positive outlook on life that our parents have. It would be a very boring life for our family if there were only one or two children, and if our parents found fault in everything around them.

Meals are served in shifts in a large room for the many returnees from the concentration camps. We still must eat in a mess hall by forming a chow line and waiting to be served. Still, Mother does not have to cook or wash dishes; isn't that great? At least now we are free to be Americans again.

We go to the other gymnasium on Sixth Street, where all our furniture and household effects were stored during the Second World War. The gymnasium, which was once filled to the ceiling, is almost bare from people removing all the valuable items, including all the reels of film and the movie projector Pop stored there. His prized outdoor motor is gone, but somehow, they did not take his valuable split bamboo fishing pole and expensive saltwater reel. Not much to salvage after almost four years of pilferage in the gymnasium that was supposed to be secured. It could be other returnees taking them as their own. We will never know. Other families have lost a great deal of material objects, but they are just objects, not lives.

There are jobs available on farms to harvest fruits and vegetables. Many works as farm hands, but my father, who was once a sharecrop farmer, has no desire to work as a farm hand, so he returns to work for Hale Brothers Department

Store as a janitor because it is steady, and the paycheck is regular. Mother is happy about Father's employment. We children must attend school because education is important. Life is now returning to normal.

We move to a basement of a house owned and lived in by a Maltese immigrant, his Czechoslovakian wife (who was born in New York) and their three children. A Japanese woman and her daughter, who is practicing being an opera singer, live in the front bedroom of the house. Do you know how difficult it is to live in the same house that has an opera student practice singing at the top of her voice? Even my mother can hear the singing, and that is saying a lot. A total of sixteen people live in this house. At least we all have shelter, but little privacy.

Granduncle Nobujiro is placed in an old-age facility where he can be properly taken care of by professionals. Father did not know where to berth him in the basement with us.

There is an old Japanese couple living in a large tent on Sixth Street while their house is being built in the front of the lot. This couple also have shelter with a kerosene lamp and stove to cook their food. This is how many Dust Bowl people lived before the Second World War just five years ago. Housing is still very hard to come by.

The basement is concrete except for my small dirt-floor cell with room enough for a cot and no other furnishings. A drop cord with a low-watt bulb illuminates the room. I can read late at night without bothering anyone. It is cold and damp in this room with one small window, where I can look at the chickens and a young pig living in a cramped space between the house and fence. It is worth going to church on Sundays to avoid the scene of a rooster being slaughtered for dinner. That is fresh meat. A suckling pig being slaughtered is a sight and sound to be avoided. Now, hunting for doves and rabbits is a different story.

The meat is gamy but good, however, the lead buck shots are a nuisance.

Two other bedrooms are bedrooms for the rest of the family, one of which belongs to my five sisters and the other for my parents and younger brother Ted. The living room is really the kitchen, dining room, living room, and a bathing area all in one. Can you imagine trying to take a bath in the living room with five sisters coming and going with their friends? I'm fifteen and can't hide anywhere, taking a bath away from the girls. Taking a shower at the school gym is my daily routine. Boy, I had more privacy in the camp!

The restroom is a small room alongside the house next to where the chickens and pigs live. I really don't want to spend too much time in there, even if it is furnished with an overhead water tank for flushing. We have returned to the Stone Age compared to the concentration camp, but we are now free. The living room door leads to a narrow alley and onto Jackson Street, the main street of Japanese Town, near Fifth Street.

Father is working steadily and providing for the family without any assistance from the Christian church that helped us during the Depression years. He buys an old pre- war car, at least ten years old, a four-door sedan, and paints it bright yellow orange. All cars are usually painted black, but no, not my father, who loves life and makes a big deal about it. He wasn't thinking about us children when he painted the car. Everyone knows Sam when he drives down the street. Not too many Japanese own a car right after the war, except my dad, and he lets everyone know it. He may be a janitor, but he owns a car, a bright yellow-orange old car he paid cash for, and everyone in town knows that. Father is unique.

Going to a beach picnic in the Santa Cruz area on a Sunday is a big affair for the family. A picnic lunch is prepared, and Dad takes us all in his bright yellow orange car. Luckily, we are all young and small, so we all fit in the car. There are seven of us kids, and Mother and Father all in the car with the picnic goodies in the spare wheel well, situated in the front fender, next to the running board. Pop also ties fishing poles on the roof and away we go.

The mountainous road to Santa Cruz twists and turns as well as steep grades up and down. I think I can get out of the car and run alongside when the car chugs uphill in first gear. What a car, but it gets us there and back. It is a good thing that the car is painted bright yellow orange, because it can be seen from afar, chugging along, making its way to the beach. It is only seventeen miles from San Jose but seems like one hundred miles. When will we ever get there? No wonder we start early in the morning, pre-dawn in fact.

At a secluded beach, a picnic is set up while Father and I do some really serious fishing for anything that will take our bait. Chunks of mackerel or sardine are our normal bait, but soft-shell sand crabs are best for the surf perch. These perches do fight more than the bullheads caught on the Santa Cruz fishing pier near the boardwalk. Bullheads open their huge mouth that is as large as their head, which is in tum larger than their body, so when you try to reel in your catch, the drag feels as though you have caught a whale or an automobile tire. Bullheads are good for throwing back into the sea unhooked, naturally. This picnic is a perfect outing for

Father because he gets to go fishing and at the same time, takes the family to the beach. Mother loves this outing because it beats staying at home in the basement.

Every morning, a friend named Bob and I walk to school early to stand guard by a tunnel leading under Fourth Street. We make sure all students walk into the tunnel instead of walking directly across the street. It is dangerous to walk across the street because the traffic flow is busy during the hours school starts and ends. Peter Burnett Junior High School is a large new school, just two short and two long blocks from home. Bob lives halfway from our home to the school.

Everyone has to get up and tell a short story in front of the class and I speak up, correcting a girl who pronounces 'aspirin' as it should. I said it should be pronounced "ah- su-pi-rin," trilling the R making a letter L sound. The class laughs at my accent and so does the teacher. I ran out of the class and went home mad and embarrassed. Here I am, a teenager born and raised in the United States, but have a strong accent in speaking English. Most teachers are tolerant of my accent. As far as I am concerned, I do not have an accent. I start to emulate other people speaking English, going as far as listening to the radio and copying them. Why didn't they tease the people who spoke differently who came from the Dust Bowl states. I couldn't get the Midwestern drawl correctly but did fine otherwise.

Father does take us all to the old Chinese restaurant on Sixth Street to eat the soft noodle chow mein with vegetables including bean sprouts mixed in, and barbecued pork sliced and placed on top. All this is served on a large serving plate.

It is like pre-war days when Pop brought us when we were young, preadolescent children. Bringing back the beautiful memory of life so long ago before the concentration camp days. As usual, Father has to go into the kitchen to talk to the Chinese workers in their dialect, probably Cantonese.

The boys upstairs and the landlord love to hunt. They invited me to hunt a small game in the country by Guadalupe Creek. We hunted for hours, but with no game to be seen. Three of us fan out and walk along the creek. A small bird flies between the two brothers, and both fire their small-bore shotguns, miss the bird, but almost end up shooting each other... friendly fire.

It is time for target practice instead of trying to shoot each other. The oldest son, John, shoots at a five-gallon can with his .410 shotgun and his brother George and I are about thirty feet away and ninety degrees from the shooter and the target. Brother George grunts, grabs his midsection, and falls to the ground. My heart is beating out of my chest, but I manage to shake him, and he awakes and says that he has been hit. No lie? No blood; he lifts his flannel shirt and there is a large red welt on his midsection where a buckshot hit him. We empty our weapons of all ammunition and call the hunting trip off and head for the barn, as they say.

A man by the name of Harry gets the city of San Jose to let him use an old firehouse on Jackson Street near First Street for a club for boys, to teach them city government and keep them occupied so they will not get into trouble at night. This club is called Boys City, and he not only put chairs and tables to hold meetings like the city, but he put in an old pool table so we can learn to play pool.

Harry finally lost the old firehouse because it became more financially profitable to tear it down and build another structure on the site.

For a while, Boys City was not in existence, but within a year Harry got another old firehouse on Julian Street near Seventh Street. Boys City was again in business, keeping young boys occupied by teaching them good city government and billiards. I cannot get the connection between the pool and city government, but I love to slide down the pole from the second floor to the main floor.

There is a numbers racket runner who happens to be an Italian American, and he doesn't run because he is lame, with one leg shorter than the other. He takes bets from Chinese gamblers, talking to them in Chinese, and writes the number down in Chinese characters. I often wonder how he takes bets from Japanese and Filipino gamblers. The police know that this person is taking bets but act as if they don't even see him. Hey, this guy is Italian in a Chinese/Japanese/ Filipino neighborhood, taking bets, and they don't see him? The police are always coming into this section of town, not to patrol but to have lunch or dinner, usually at a Chinese restaurant and walk out without paying one red cent. The police, like the numbers racket runner, are not seen by the restaurant workers when they walk out either. Everyone is blind and mute, but corruption goes on because it is easier this way than being harassed every day.

The Shinto shrine (temple) finally has concreted the basement and made the spaces livable for us to move into. We just need a larger living space than this basement we are in now, with the cramped spaces and minimum of conveniences available, and the Shinto shrine is perfect, with a full bathroom by itself. However, the rooms are darker because the sunlight does not enter the lower portion of the house. It is gloomy here in the temple basement. Although it is several blocks away from Japanese Town, it is closer to San Jose High School on San Fernando Street. Soon my sisters will be attending high school with me.

The priest and his family live in the rear section of the house, and the large living room serves as the temple area for the Shinto services. They have a large victory garden that is well kept, except along the neighbor's fence, where the neighbor throws their trash and garbage. The neighbors hate Japanese, and this is one way to express their hatred. The priest and the family don't complain, but I see their hurt. They just bury the garbage and bum the trash. There is no bitterness in life, only in the green tea we drink to remind us that sometimes life is bitter.

Father brings home an opossum in a gunny sack and ties the sack to a tree in the backyard near the garage. We have never seen an opossum and he explained about it, especially the function of its tail and the pouch it has. He says that it tastes very good as a stew, and he plans to make opossum stew for us tomorrow. This doesn't go over well for us children, who think the animal looks much like a large rat. Who would enjoy eating any animal that looks like a rat with an ugly, hairless tail? In the morning, the sack has a large hole, and the opossum is nowhere in sight. Father knew that the opossum would chew itself out of a gunny sack but didn't want us to know.

What a relief, no rat stew tonight. Did my sisters release the opossum?

Sunday fishing trips for Father and me have become more frequent. He doesn't take my sisters, because he says it is a man's thing, but I'm sure that at least one of my sisters would like to come along just for the ride. He wakes me early in the morning before dawn and off we go. Stop near the First Street Post Office at a small cafe with a high ceiling, a long counter with stools and along the narrow room are several small tables with chairs. Father orders hotcakes and coffee for both of us. The cook is generous with butter and pure maple syrup for the stack of three fluffy hotcakes. This cafe is open twenty-four hours a day, and there are people eating, or drinking coffee all the time. Soon we are on the road to Santa Cruz, hoping to get there just before the sun rises. Fishing is best one hour before sunrise, according to Father. I always wonder how fish can see in the dark of the day prior to sunup.

When we returned one day from our fishing trip, there was huge party going on upstairs in the Shinto Shrine. Long tables with food and drinks are available for the guests. A lady gives me a drink in a large eight-ounce glass from a quart-size 7-Up bottle. Being dehydrated from the fishing trip, I gulp almost half of the drink and it burns my throat. I swallow half and spit the other out. The lady finds that someone has put sake, a rice wine, in the large 7-Up bottle. Pop gets really upset about me being served sake. It was a mistake, and no one is at fault. Hungry as I am and thirsty at that, the little sake which I have consumed makes me dizzy, and off to bed I go without supper or bath, and the only regret is going to bed smelling fishy.

Neither that incident nor the neighbors made us move around the block to our "new" home. Father has bought a

house of our own. This is a dream come true for our parents to own their own home. It is an old Victorian house with three large bedrooms, a living room, large dining room with a fireplace, large kitchen we use as dining area and pantry room that is large, with windows and a sink. There is a large basement with windows at ground level. The basement is used as a storage area. We sure have collected a lot of things since returning to San Jose carrying a few suitcases. Housing is still critical in San Jose, but Father did not make the basement available to other families in need. It did not have adequate living spaces like a separate toilet or kitchen facilities. My parents did not want other people to live in this environment, because they have suffered living in substandard housing before.

Learn The Traditions
Traditions and cultures must be kept alive

When we first moved into our own home, Father emphasized the importance of maintaining and participating in the Japanese tradition and culture. This is probably the reason why my parents have always spoken Japanese to us. Many immigrants continue to hold on to their old traditions and customs, because they do not want to lose part of their homeland and heritage. When the language is lost, traditions and customs are lost. Once the traditions are lost, their ties to the homeland disappear. It is difficult for me to understand some of the Japanese traditions because they go back centuries and have religious connotations. After being a Christian for many years, and never having any other religious teaching, following the Japanese traditions with Buddhist and Shinto histories is difficult to understand.

There are other cultures in the United States that follow their traditions, and some of them, in my opinion, are really disastrous to the family finances, especially for the poor. Most immigrants coming to the United States are poor and are starting a new life with limited finances and language barriers. Thus, immigrants are often given work that is menial, with minimum wages at most. Some work in sweatshops, which don't exist to the law enforcers. Some employees in these sweatshops are undocumented immigrants who can be deported if caught working, so they keep quiet and a low profile.

Immigrants are here to live a new life, but really do not want to forget where they came from and the customs of their land. Many fled their country because of political or financial reasons. If they remained in their land, their life is in jeopardy. They do not want to totally forget the old times and old traditions. Old traditions should be followed, so that they are not forgotten, but not at the expense of alienating the culture from modem thoughts. Modem mores should never dilute the traditional conservative lifestyle.

To forget your traditions and customs is to lose your identity. When you are from four different cultures-as some of my grandnephews and nieces are-you are an American with mixed, wonderful life and cultures.

The Obon-odori festival of the Buddhist Church of San Jose, California has yearly street dancing in front of the temple. It is a joyous and colorful event with traditional music, including the drumbeat, so the dancers can keep in step, as well as moving their arms and body to the rhythm. The reverberations of the drum woke up the primeval emotions within me and probably many other bystanders listening and watching the event as well. However, the Obon is really honoring the dead.

Kimonos are either bought or made by the women and girls for this occasion. The expensive silk kimonos are proudly worn by some of the wealthier women, and more often, colorful cotton print ones are made at home instead. The Buddhist church has dance practices for many months prior to the festival, so that everyone, including men and boys, knows the dance steps and hand movements. The males wear their hapi coats and join in. As for me, I have never joined in. This is one tradition strictly dominated by the Buddhist church where I have to pass. Going to Japan Town on Obonodori night is always an exciting experience that I can observe from the sidelines with the rest of the crowd. Food and soft drinks are sold at the gymnasium for a nominal fee. Obon dances are fine to gather the community together to enjoy the festival, and to keep old traditions alive without disrupting current affairs or mores.

My parents never encouraged us to participate in the Obon festival, because we did work with our parents every night from six to nine o'clock, and Sunday mornings until noon. Dance practice was held during the evening hours and weekends. Buying silk kimonos for five young ladies in our household is rather expensive. Mother has her own silk kimono, including one black formal kimono with a mon (family crest of three butterflies circling three commas) for special occasions. These are folded neatly and stored in the clothes closet.

One tradition in this area is that whenever someone dies in the Japanese community who is family or a friend, a small cash donation is given to that family. This family records who donated and the amount. A thank-you note will be given later. Whenever this family has a friend or family member die, the record is referred to, and the same amount of money is donated to that other family. This probably carried on for centuries. The reason was never explained to me; however, in the early 1900s, when the Japanese immigrated to this country and the person died, that family had a difficult time raising money for the funeral.

The small donation from other Japanese helped defray the cost of the funeral. This is a wonderful tradition. Flowers are also given along with the cash donation and noted as well in the record book. This tradition is still carried out. Whenever there is a death in a family, seems the family drifts away from each other only to regroup as a smaller but a different family structure.

Baishakunin is a matchmaker for family weddings. This is where one person will approach a family to arrange a marriage. Father and I visit a farmer who has a young lady of marriageable age. I guess Father has some idea that I should be getting married or thinking of marriage. While Father and the farmer are talking, the young lady and I were left alone to discuss what they were discussing. Both of us are embarrassed at what is happening because we have never met before, nor have we been planning on getting married, especially to each other. We made a decision to tell our fathers that we are not interested in their plans for our future. The young lady probably has her eyes on someone else, and I have no plans for marriage, or for settling down to raise a family.

Everyone knows that this meeting is not going well, so our fathers tell us to think about it and let them know later. We have never let them know because we never did change our minds. This is not a good tradition for parents to make their children marry someone they have never met, nor someone who is picked as a spouse by a marriage arranger. Some marriages are made to stop a family feud or unite two powerful families into one. Other marriages are made for financial or property gain. These marriages are not of one person loving another and living happily ever after. The saying goes, "They will eventually fall in love with each other."

In some cultures, the marriage is pre-arranged when the two are still children. These children know who their spouse will be, years prior to the actual wedding date. Can you imagine knowing that so-and-so will be my future spouse and he or she will look like their old parents? Can you imagine that it is impossible to get out of this pre-arranged marriage because it is "till death do us part" years before you get married? Your fate has been sealed and there is no room for change. I guess the man could join a foreign legion and then get a French citizenship and move to Paris to get out of the marriage. Ah, yes, Paris the city of lights and action.

Japanese New Year is celebrated on regular American New Year's Day but traditionally runs for three days. Traditionally, prior to the New Year, Japanese business owners give all their employees a special bonus. This bonus is used to pay all debts that have accumulated during the year, and the new year is started with a clean slate. This is another wonderful tradition; however, today, debts are not cleared yearly, because bonuses are not given to employees in the United States, and debts are not realistic.

Celebrating for three days is a big burden for any family, especially when people are coming over constantly giving gifts, as well as consuming well-prepared food and drinking lots of hot sake while singing songs. It gets to be a contest when one tries to outdo another, and that is bad. Today, a traditional New Year's meal consists of the old Japanese feast and some Western food all brought as potluck by family members to defray the cost of the huge feast but only last one meal. This is one big buffet dinner lasting several hours. The whole family meets together for a meal at least once a year to get reacquainted.

The fortunate people are the Buddhists, who do not have to buy Christmas gifts. They do not have to buy any Christmas gifts on credit. If they buy these gifts on credit, then by tradition they must pay the credit off prior to New Year's Day, and that will be just weeks or even days away. Isn't this a stressful situation?

Every Japanese family of years ago prepares a large feast using all the vegetables and seafood they can. Such vegetables are bamboo shoots, gobo (burdock), taro roots, water lily plants, black beans, red beans, water chestnuts, etc. The sea foods are sea cucumbers, seaweed made into a bow tie, herring roe, sea urchin roe, salmon roe, broiled carp, sashimi, etc. Can you imagine buying all the strange foods at the local market? This all must last for three days, because the people will be visiting each house bringing gifts of shoyu, dried persimmons, fresh fruits, rice, sake, etc. Beer and sake flow freely, and there is happiness in the air because they are all starting the New Year debt free and one year older.

Father buys two large wood mallets, bamboo rice steamers, a large marble formed with a depression for pounding rice etc. to make mochi the traditional way. The rice is steamed and pounded by Bob and me, while Father turns the rice so it will be pounded evenly. Mother and my sisters shape the pounded rice into round and oval mochi of different varieties. The first batch of the plain mochi is offered to the Buddhist and Shinto shrines at home. Father teaches us how to make mochi the old traditional way, because soon all mochi will be machine-made and will not have the essences or the taste of the traditional mochi. In fact, he does say that the mochi will be made from rice flour. Did you know that the old mochi has the hint of smoke from the wood fire to heat the water into steam?

Yes, one year older. Father tells me that since I spent nine months with Mother prior to being born, that is considered one year, and on New Year's Day, I become another year older. Since I was born in September 1933, I am already one year old and in January 1934, am now two years old instead of three months old. It really gets confusing to me, because in January 1934 I should be one year old. Father said that we are aged just like horses are aged. A yearling becomes one year old on the first New Year's Day. He must have been kidding around with me. Anyway, birthdays are easier to celebrate because everyone becomes a year older on New Year's. One big party is being celebrated for both. Can you imagine having a birthday party almost every month in our family alone?

My parents never discuss going to Japan for a religious retreat or a pilgrimage but only to visit old relatives. There is a tradition that one must climb Mount Fuji near Tokyo once in their lifetime to see the sun rise on the country called "the land of the rising sun." But we Japanese Americans have no reason to do that, except only because the volcano is there to climb. It is a volcano, and it may wake at any time without warning, and it is not very wise to be climbing such a hazardous peak unless you want to prove something. It is even unwise to live near that mountain at any time. The sleeping giant may awaken, and what a place that area will be! Mother does encourage me to visit the city of Hiroshima and see firsthand the huge damage that the atomic bomb has done in August 1945.

Religious retreats or pilgrimages are stressed by religious leaders so we can "meet our religious obligations," and they often lead large groups to training camps or religious sites such as Mecca, Jerusalem, the Vatican, Fatima, or even the Ganges River. It is great to go on these trips if you can afford it, but you should never feel obligated, especially when you have to borrow from the bank. Many traditions and religious obligations are man-made, even the church stresses following them, but to me, it is still man-made. Remember, the leader of a large group going on a trip goes gratis. Any tour company will give one free seat for a large group on a tour initiated by that person.

In other cultures, there is a tradition when a young lady becomes fifteen years old, and they have a comingout party called a "quinceanera. "A beautiful wedding gown is purchased for her and also for her friends. Young men approximately her same age is given tuxedos to wear for the occasion. More often, this formalwear is rented for the day, except the young lady's gown. A professional photographer is hired for still photos, video and digital. Usually, the family gathers at the local church and has the priest or pastor hold services and give his blessings at a cost. After the services, all friends and relatives gather at a rented hall and have a feast that has been catered and dance all night long to a live band or disc jockey. This traditional fifteenth birthday for the young lady will cost just as much as a wedding will cost when she gets married a few years later.

A family really wants to have this party, but usually they cannot afford such a large traditional affair, especially for a single mom. Some go into debt by mortgaging their homes, and many more borrow from many friends and relatives to make even a small get together. I come from a family of five ladies, and luckily our culture does not have this coming-out party sanctioned and encouraged by the church or temple. Church leaders are to spread their beliefs on religion or philosophy, not to encourage having a huge party just because someone has turned fifteen years old. It is all about money. Priests, caterers, disc jockeys or musical bands, wedding gown and tuxedo shops, limousines, florists, and church halls all stand to make money. Will they discourage such a money-making affair? After all, thousands of dollars are involved. Many traditionalists encourage this coming-out party, but do not contribute to funding or assisting in the fete. They do want to join in the festivities of eating, drinking, and dancing, at the expense of the family of the debutante. Who is brainwashed in this tradition? I love to attend the fifteenth-year parties. Is a bar or bat mitzvah any different?

A friend explains that as a young fifteen-year-old girl, her single mother had a coming-out party with all the trimmings, and she remembers it all to this date. It is so beautiful and memorable that she will never forget the thrill of it for the rest of her life. She is lucky because she is the only child of a working mother. She is unemployed, as is her husband, but had a coming-out party for her youngest daughter. This was held at a Roman Catholic church at

Rosarito Beach, just south of Tijuana, Mexico. The daughter will never forget this occasion and will remember the sacrifice of her parents to make this event happen.

Traditions of various cultures are made by men and not by God or a Supreme Being. We have our own traditional holidays, such at New Year's Day to watch the Rose Bowl Parade and game; Presidents' Day to rest on that Monday or have a nice barbecue; Easter Sunday to attend the sunrise services then hunt for eggs with the children; Memorial Day to honor the dead and have another nice barbecue; Independence Day, once called Fourth of July, to celebrate our breakaway from English rule and have another nice barbecue; Thanksgiving Day to celebrate the first Thanksgiving with the American Indians during the 1600s and have a nice feast of roast turkey; Christmas Day to celebrate Christ's birth and to exchange gifts.

Those are the traditional holidays set down according to the Americans but there are many more, such as: Martin Luther King's birthday, Groundhog Day, Valentine's Day, St. Patrick's Day, Palm Sunday, Passover, Labor Day, Rosh Hashanah, Yorn Kippur, Columbus Day, Veterans' Day, Ramadan, Hanukkah, and Kwanzaa, to name just a few. Many are religious and some do celebrate an occasion or someone's birthday in order that we as a cultural society do not forget these important days, but we really shouldn't press our cultural events upon others who are opposed to it.

Knowing the language helps keep the culture, customs, and traditions alive. It is the obligation of all Americans to have love and understanding toward others. We all must be tolerant.

Summer Vacation
It is now harvest time

As soon as possible, even before summer vacation, my siblings and I are taken to a raspberry patch to harvest. We pick only the ripe berries and place them in a can. They are later counted and placed in a lug box full of berry baskets. Each can is worth money, and we are later paid the amount we have picked. Blackberries and boysenberries are picked. The monies earned are to be our allowance, instead of Father using his wages for our needs. This is the start of our typical summer vacation.

Later, I found a job picking cherries at Mr. M's orchard. He tries to get me to harvest his radishes and other row crops, but I find that the work is bothering my back, so I quit. Picking cherries using an extension (snake) ladder, several hooks, and two metal pails enables me to gather many more cherries with one ladder setting than using a regular three-legged one.

Near the end of the season, the uppermost part of the cherry trees has the most fruit, because pickers avoid the height, especially when the breeze picks up. I like it up there, because after tying the ladder securely, I can pick a lot of the ripe cherries, and often these are so ripe, they are fermenting and shriveling up. They are sweet, with lots of sugar content. I eat these, and with the breeze swaying the ladder to and fro, the fermented cherries are working, and I am one happy cherry picker.

As soon as the cherry season ends, apricot season starts, and Mr. S. near the foothills of East San Jose hires me to pick his 'cots. He teaches me to drive his flatbed Model T Ford truck, but there are no seats for driver and passenger. I have to drive standing up, and there are three pedals on the floor. One is the gas, one is the brake, and the other is used for backing up. Just below the steering wheel on the column are several levers for spark, gas, choke, etc.

Mr. S. has two spare engines sitting on wooden blocks on a long workbench, ready to replace the engine in the Ford truck when the engine fails to operate. He fixes the spare engines during the winter months and will have them ready for the spring harvest.

Instead of me picking apricots for shipping and drying, I drive the truck around, picking up boxes of ripe fruit to be sorted at the farm barn. The ripe apricots which cannot be shipped will be cut by the ladies and laid on a large, flat drying tray cut side up. These trays are stacked on a dolly, ready to be rolled on rails to a smoke shed. After being pushed into the smoke shed, a mound of yellow sulfur is burned and the shed tightly sealed, keeping the sulfur smoke in the room as a preservative for the apricots, so the fruits will not discolor. The sulfur may also be used to keep the flies from contaminating the fruit.

Once, I went back into a tree full of ripe apricots and the fruits fell to the ground. The 'cots were gathered into a box and turned in to Mr. S., explaining what had happened. He has never reprimanded me for my failings. My father always told me to work hard no matter what, to show up for work ahead of time, never miss a day of work, be honest, and never complain about the work. I guess this is the reason Mr. Stein likes me as a worker.

After the fruits have been curing in the smoke shed, the dolly is rolled out and moved to the drying area. We lay the trays side by side in an open field so the apricots can dry. I have not seen one fly in the area. This is a no-fly zone.

I turn all my checks that are earned as a farm laborer over to Father, who banks them for me. This is my allowance money for anything that is needed, including clothes. My sisters earn allowance money by picking berries. We are allowed to buy almost anything we need, and when we want it, we ask Father for the money. This helps the family finances and allows Father to save for our own house somewhere eventually, but probably here near Japanese Town. My parents dream of their own home, even though they know it is difficult saving money while raising seven children.

Picking prunes is not a job for me. San Jose people were once called prune pickers because there were many prune orchards in San Jose. I don't know how prune pickers can be on their hands and knees or bent over all day long, picking ripe plums off the ground and putting them into a lug box. These plums are dipped into a solution of lye and then laid on a drying tray and set out into the bright sun. The farmer offered me twenty-five cents a box. I picked all day long and did not pick a box, so I gave the plums to my sister. One of the rules is to show up early for work. Sorry, I didn't show up, I quit.

Mr. E.S. has at least one hundred acres of pears. The first pick is by his farmhouse. Bartletts are picked for shipping first, then later for the canneries. Buyers will make a bid to buy the crop by the ton. The price will be set after the buyer plugs several pears and reads the sugar content of the pears.

We use sizing rings to ensure the fruits are all of legal size. The last bartlett picking is for baby foods and every fruit is stripped from the trees regardless of the sugar content. The baby food canneries will buy even the very small fruit that I would throw on the ground for mulch. Mr. Sakauye has Asian pears, Anjous, cornice, winter nellis, etc.

His fruits were much sought-after by shipping buyers because they are blue ribbon winners at the Santa Clara County Fair. Although many of the pear pickers on Mr. Sakauye's orchard are Japanese Americans, he does have several contract braceros. Braceros come from Mexico to help harvest crops in the United States, and they are contracted to work, and a portion of their pay is given to the contractor for room and board. They are crowded ten to twenty in a house, given three meals a day, and driven to a job site by the contractor.

A bracero is given two burritos for his lunch. Bean burritos are the usual fare but sometimes cheese is added as a bonus. Can you imagine eating two bean burritos every noon hour for lunch? One bracero likes to exchange his burritos for my two bologna sandwiches. Each bracero is happy to work in the United States because the working conditions 1n Mexico are terrible and the pay is extremely low.

Two Mexican ladies and a sixteen-year-old girl live in their large, older-model car while they work as fruit pickers. These women, the mother, her daughter, and an aunt, travel from Texas at the start of harvest season in early spring for cherries and will work the fruit harvest until near end of October or November, then travel back to Texas. My young daughter has not attended school now for several years because she needs to earn money to help support the family. They have told me that they make enough money in six months in California that the rest of the six months in Texas is leisure time to be with their family. Seriously, I think that they live in Mexico, not Texas. To them, working for survival is more important than a good education.

Three people living in a car is difficult, but when you have to do this to survive, you must tolerate hardships. Cooking, washing clothes, taking baths, and even trying to keep warm during the cool evenings is difficult under the harsh living conditions. They keep to themselves, not getting friendly with other male pickers, but seem to be enjoying their migrant life. At least they have the apparent protection from the orchard owner on their personal safety by living close to the farmhouse.

When I experience life working along with migrant workers, I am glad to have what little I have, especially going home every day to a warm house, hot wholesome food, hot bath, a clean, soft bed, and the company of my loving family. The years in the concentration camp have taught me to be tolerant of hardships and be appreciative of what little I have.

There are many people in California who are working hard to make ends meet because they are put in that position to be poor. There are people who must stop attending school just to help feed the family. This is wrong; everyone must and should finish high school. Children must never be exploited to help feed the family. Many third world countries are exploiting their children to the point where the country will never be productive in this modem world because of lack of education. Often, this is not the fault of the parents; it is a society of the ruling class that wants uneducated workers to be the majority where they, the wealthy, can live off the labors of the uneducated poor people. Slavery in a sense has not disappeared and thrives today.

Our parents are not exploiting us in the family by encouraging us to go out and work during the summer vacation. If we do not keep active by honest work, we may be keeping busy doing things that may be wrong. All the money we have given to Father is accounted for in his book, so we know exactly how much we have at any given time. It is our money to spend.

When I was fifteen, Father gave me permission to hire on as a field hand to a vineyard in Lodi, California. There is a guardian who travels with me on an old flatbed stake truck from San Jose. It is his responsibility to keep me out of harm's way. At fifteen years old, I am about the naivest boy alive, but anxious to learn about working outside of Santa Clara Valley, away from my family, under the care of a grandfatherly man.

Father gives me a German-made straight razor, leather strop, honing stone, shaving mug with soap inside, and a shaving brush. He tells me that I am now a man and need this shaving kit to shave off my peach fuzz on my face. I must be always clean-shaven. Just looking at the sharp and shiny razor makes me nervous, too nervous to shave.

We arrive at the bunkhouse, where all the grape pickers are housed. There are two bunkhouses, all occupied by Japanese men. The agreement is that we live here and will be fed three meals a day, but a portion of the daily pay will be deducted for board and room. We will be paid hourly wages, which are higher than the going minimum wage.

The bunkhouse is a long, single-room wooden building with many windows and several doors. Air flows freely here, thank goodness, because Lodi during the harvest season is hot and humid. I am assigned a cot with a footlocker at the foot of the bed. All my clothes and toilet articles are stored in the locker.

There is a wooden hot tub large enough to accommodate four people at one time, where we all have to bathe every night after work. First, we water down our bodies with water, and scrub with soap and a towel. Then comes the rinsing part where water is poured over the head to remove the soap from the head and body. This is all done outside the tub, ensuring that the hot tub water always stays clean. The water is so hot that I have to ease myself into the tub and then slowly sit down and soak. All this soaking removes the aches and pains, and I am ready to work again. For the older Japanese workers, this hot tub, Jura, is an old traditional bath and very therapeutic.

The meals are served in a large room with several long tables and benches to accommodate all the workers at one time. This is like eating in the concentration camp, but here, all the food is placed in large bowls and plates in the center of the table, where we can reach and serve ourselves. Seconds are encouraged if hungry. Usually it is eggs, rice, hotcakes, potatoes, bacon, and toast for breakfast. For lunch and dinner, it is rice, cooked vegetables, with bits of meat and soup. The meals are always different, so we won't be bored. Coffee is served for breakfast and tea is served at every meal. To me, this is comfort food Japanese style, but still reminds me of camp.

The first morning at the vineyard bunkhouse, I awakened early, well before sunrise, and told to wash up and get ready to eat and to work. I go to the bathhouse, where there is a wooden walkway completely around it with water spigots every yard or so. This is where everyone washes their face, shaves, and brushes their teeth. It is dark here, no lights and no sunlight, but enough light from the bunkhouse to move around without bumping into each other. Now, how can I shave with my new straight razor in this condition? I don't see other men shaving, so they must have shaven the night before when there was available light.

I am given a pruning shears and instructed how to snip the ripe and only ripe grapes off the vine and lay them in a lug box neatly, ready for shipping. After filling a lug box, I take it to a ladder, and he nails a lid on it and stacks it with the rest of the boxes.

It is Friday the ninth of September 1949, early in the afternoon, and we are driven back to the bunkhouse because the owner/boss is observing his religious belief of not working and observing the Sabbath. This is my birthday, turning sixteen years old. The flatbed stake truck is traveling thirty-five miles per hour in the left lane, heading north toward Lodi on Highway 99, ready to make a left turn.

There are several men, including a boy my age, sitting at the end of the bed, dangling their feet. The tailgate is not in place to keep everyone enclosed in the bed of the truck. I, a typical young lad, am playing around on the bed and putting grapes down a thirty-three-year-old medical student's back.

Another stake truck is trying to pass us in the dirt center divider to the highway. The driver comes alongside, and he knows he could not pass us, so he turns his wheels to the right and sideswipes our truck, causing five of us to fall off the truck. The thirty-three-year-old medical student falls on his head on the highway and dies several hours later at the Lodi hospital. An old man breaks his collar bone, another breaks a leg, the sixteen-year-old escapes injuries and I have road burns on my left cheek, elbows, and knees. I landed on my feet, but the momentum made me roll many times and eventually come to a scraping halt.

After I was patched up, the doctor asked if I was all right. How can I be all right when I was spending several hours in the same room as the thirty-three-year-old medical student, watching him slowly die? I'm a sixteen-year-old kid and I'm not all right, all right!

One week later, after sitting around at the bunkhouse, the doctor releases me and I'm on my way home via the Greyhound Bus Line. When I arrive at the basement of the Fifth and Jackson Street home, I knock on the door and Mother opens it and she asks what I want. What do I want? I'm Bobby, your son, who came home.

She did not recognize me because of the bandage on my face and being completely sunburned from working the grape harvest without a shirt on or a hat. Mother said that she read about the tragic accident in Lodi from the Japanese newspaper, but she thought that Robert Saito was another person. How many Robert

Saitos are in the Lodi area? Anyway, everyone including Mother calls me Bobby.

Mr. G, who runs the concession at the Civic Auditorium in town, hires me to sell sodas, ice cream, popcorn, peanuts, you name it during the weekly wrestling and boxing matches. There are special occasions such as basketball games, including the Harlem Globetrotters that I worked at night and usually was home by ten o'clock, earning an easy nine dollars in about three hours, when the hourly wages are about $1.25.

He hires me for the county fair during September, just before school season. This helps cook hamburgers, onions, hot dogs, and even come on the cob. We all have fun working at a fast pace, keeping up with the needs of our customers. It has been known that hamburgers were given out without meat. This is our original veggie burger. We work from the time the gates open until closing time. Our pay is well above the minimum wage, and we are also fed. Often we eat on the run, as they say, fast food. This is my usual summer vacation, as well as my sisters', earning our allowances, freeing our parents from financial burden by us.

Our Own House
Our parents' dream comes true

Father buys me a 1936 Plymouth sedan and tells me that when he became a man, his father gave him a horse. This day and age, a horse is not used for transportation in the city. Although our garage was a stable and carriage storage area at one time, we cannot use it for that purpose today. One condition is to take my sisters to high school with me in the morning. After school, my sisters walk home because I practice for the swimming and water polo team under the coaching of Rudy.

Father has already taken the San Jose Water Works as his own contract to clean daily. Mother and three of us older children assist him in cleaning the building daily, Mondays through Fridays, from six to nine at night. My parents will continue until about midnight to finish. We all take a short snack break at about nine o'clock, and this usually consists of rice balls and pickles with tea. After the evening snack, I drive to my sister's home. The other children would help occasionally. Sunday nights, Father and I would check on the office building and do some spot cleaning or window washing if someone has come to work and dirtied the spaces during the weekend. All trash is burned in the incinerator located at the rear of the buildings. Nothing is left to accumulate. Father now has his own janitorial business and is doing rather well with it.

When Father first came to the United States, Asians could not own any property or attend public schools. This, in a way, kept the Asians uneducated, poor, and non-property owners. The wonderful land of the free and opportunity did not apply to the Asians. The Great Depression of the 1930s rocked the whole nation into poverty, except a few rich people who grew richer from the suffering of the laboring poor. World War II became the years of uncertainty for Father, because he didn't know what will happen to us while we are in a concentration camp. The two atomic bombs that were dropped on Japan and killed over a hundred thousand people, including women and children, brought the war to a rapid end. Who can win a war against such devastating bombs? Hard times hounded Father from the 1920s until 1950, but we never went without food or warm clothing, except that first day of arrival at Heart Mountain War Relocation Center in Wyoming in September 1942, while the biting cold zipped through our scantily clad bodies.

Four years after being released from the concentration camp with nothing to his name, Father now owns a car, his own janitor business, and a house to call his own. He came a long way with Mother. This is our own house. He bought the house for Mother and us kids to live in. Julian was born in November 1950. Our parents, with a very large family, now have made it where many others are still struggling, living in substandard housing, paying rent.

Father and Mother work side-by-side as much as possible the traditional, old-fashioned way. They are the ones who laid down the foundation of our lives. We were never without food, clothing, or shoes. Although we lived in a farmhouse, an old house without electricity, several barracks in camps, temporary shelter at a Buddhist temple, a crowded basement, and a basement in a Shinto temple, we were never homeless, but the living conditions were not ideal.

Now we are living in our own warm, cozy, large house, all ten of us, with enough rice to last us until the new crop comes out in the fall. This year, Dad has bought seventeen sacks of new-crop rice each sack weighing one hundred pounds, and gallons of Kikkoman shoyu. He also buys many cans of floor wax; each can hold five gallons of wax for his business. Even soap and tri-sodium phosphate are purchased by the fifty-five-gallon container and stored at the San Jose Water Works and California Water Works on Santa Clara Street across from Bridgeman's Recreation Center, a bowling alley. Everything is purchased as much as possible in bulk so Father can get that huge discount.

Everyone who is old enough to work is busy during the weekends, helping Father with his janitorial business. I eat my lunch at Wes' Cafe across the street from San Jose High School on San Fernando Street. My comer of operation is near the loud jukebox selling sandwiches, Coke, and pre- cooked hamburgers.

As soon as we move into the house, a telephone is installed, and this is the first telephone that our family has owned. The phone number: Cypress 5-6313 is memorized by all. Sister Amy buys a television with an antenna attached onto our steep roof, and now our old Victorian home has become a twentieth-century house with modem appliances. Even our stove, refrigerator, and washing machine are brand new. This is our house, so warm and cozy. Mother and Father's dream has come true.

Pioneer
Nobujiro Saito

Nobujiro Saito is the first of the Saito family to arrive in the United States, about 1900. Son to the Saitos of Hiroshima, Japan, born 1876. He may have heard and read about the great Gold Rush of California, where men were picking up huge nuggets from stream beds, earning them lots of money. These stories about the 1848 Gold Rush were greatly exaggerated, but it stirred the hearts of many men and set them to daydream; Nobujiro may have been one.

Another gold rush of the Yukon Territory and Alaska of 1899 reaches worldwide, and again men are rushing to claim their wealth. The extreme hardship in getting to the gold fields is downplayed, and many people have their hopes on that gold.

Nobujiro, as the second son, is not an heir to the Saito family land, and he must either work for the family as a servant or strike out on his own to earn his property. We really do not know all his history, but a postcard is received dated 1906 that he is needed and requested to return to a gold camp in Alaska. Nobujiro, in his late twenties, was already working at a gold camp in Alaska in the early 1900s. Since he is an Asian and looks like an Inuit, he was probably hired as a servant or cook. Inuit are despised in Alaska, as

Native Americans are hated in the United States at that time. Nobujiro surely could not have been a miner under these conditions.

I believe that our granduncle Nobujiro was a cook at the camp, because he is the best baker of sourdough bread I have ever met. His hot sourdough bread just melts in my mouth whenever I have the pleasure of eating it. He always has a large pot of soup or stew on the old cast iron wood- burning stove for anyone who is hungry, and that includes the hobos who often come to our back door for a handout.

Before I was born in 1933, there was an article in the Japanese newspaper that Nobujiro Saito is looking for his brother or nephew living in California; he is destitute and unable to seek employment because of his arthritis. He is already over fifty years old, and that is considered old currently. My grandfather passed on in Los Angeles, and father gets word of his uncle's plight.

Father goes to Seattle, Washington, pays uncle's debts, and brings him to the farm at Berryessa, California, near San Jose. I met an old Japanese man in a bar in Seattle during the early 1970s, and he has heard of Nobujiro Saito and his hardship. Although Seattle has Japanese living in the area, the community is not large, and everyone knows each other or has heard stories about members of their community. Since Nobujiro 's arrival in the United States, he has spent most of his time in Seattle, instead of the gold mining camp of Alaska.

Granduncle has been my primary babysitter since birth because Mom is busy with twins born in 1935, then many more children thereafter. In every picture of Granduncle, he is dressed in a suit with a tie, even when he is babysitting.

Although he was always in pain because of arthritis, his smile is there as though the world is a bright and happy place to be. You would never suspect all the hardship he must have had, working under extreme bitter conditions in Alaska during the early 1900s. Granduncle is very happy that Father has taken him in the family and is now caring for him while Granduncle cares for me.

Japanese who have immigrated to the United States have not really passed down stories to the younger generation of their hardships in a new land of opportunity. Many are bachelors or single persons who came to our wonderful land and worked hard to survive, often sending money back to their home in Japan to support the family they have left behind. Like many immigrants who have come to America, they have supported family members in their homeland. Nobujiro and other immigrants all had colorful lives and did not pass them down; nor have they written accounts of daily life. A few stories have surfaced but not enough.

I write this short account of Nobujiro Saito so my nephews and nieces and their children can have a history of our first pioneer to America. He must have been a daring young man of his mid-twenties, coming to a strange land, not knowing the English language, and having limited cash in pocket. In another words, he is a typical young immigrant to America, seeking riches and fortune in 1900.

He must have had high hopes, arriving in Seattle, Washington, probably trying to get to the gold fields in Alaska or the Yukon Territory. One prospective gold miner had to have money to survive and return. Many returned with horrible experiences of the trek and mining that really did not produce riches for them. Some have perished, leaving no account of their life struggles. Somehow, Nobujiro managed to get to a mining camp in Alaska and worked.

Many communities, Seattle included, had rooming houses for Japanese men and women to stay at while waiting for employment or wintering over between jobs. These rooming houses often had a kitchen and dining room for their guests. Nobujiro stayed at these rooming houses often, up until about 1930. For thirty years, he worked in the mining camps of Alaska and in Seattle as either a cook or baker. I doubt that he has ever worked in the timber industry or the fishing industry of the Pacific Northwest.

Granduncle Nobujiro was at Santa Anita Assembly Center in Southern California from March to August 1942, and at Heart Mountain, Wyoming Relocation Center until the end of the Second World War in 1945. He was berthed separate from our family because the federal government considered him a single man. He no longer became part of our family because he lived in a different block from us. The harsh winters of Wyoming took a toll on his physical health because he had a very hard time moving around.

Upon his return to San Jose, California, Nobujiro could no longer move freely, and my father had to carry him. Father found an old age home for Granduncle. For several years, he lived at home, in a single room, bare except for a large cross above his bed. This is a Roman Catholic cross, another mystery of his past; a hidden religion, because Christians were persecuted in Japan when he was a young boy.

The Saitos of Japan are Shinto in their beliefs, so he may have converted after he left Japan.

Father and I visited Nobujiro often, bringing him small gifts of food, and naturally, cigars. He loves to smoke cigars, especially the Red Dot brand, which is sweet to the taste. His smile is always there, happy to see us, as he is ageing and unable to walk.

Granduncle Nobujiro Saito passed on in 1948 at the age of seventy-two, an old age at this time. He hasn't told or written about his life, which must have been exciting at the time of the years 1876 to 1948. A lot of things happened during this period, including the great Gold Rush of 1899, World War I, the Great Depression, World War II, and the atomic age. How did he live day by day during these years?

Apparently, he was a Roman Catholic, but his funeral service was at the Buddhist temple, and he was cremated. The ashes are sent to Japan, where he will be with his family.

Forgotten but not alone

When I leave this earth,

gather my bones and ashes

from the just cool' d hearth

bury them with my family

who has passed ahead.

Carve my name on a bare stone

this will be my bed.

Although I' 11 be forgotten,

my name is in stone

gathering moss 'neath cool trees but I'll not be 'lone.

My bones and ashes buried

'neath gray granite stone

may last least one thousand years my soul and spirit

is resting in peace not 'lone.

Sam Shunji Saito
1899-1969

Like Granduncle Nobujiro Saito, my father did not talk about his colorful life. I say colorful because of what was learned about him from snips of his talks and from other people who knew him. It is strange that people who do have a colorful life seldom talk about themselves. They are not embarrassed or shy about it; they just believe it is not that important to them or anyone else. I say it is important to their families who are curious and want to know about the family's past. Wouldn't you love to learn about your father's or mother's life?

There are many stories of immigrants who arrived in the United States with a few cents in their pockets but a determination to succeed in a strange land full of opportunities. These are the stories that are interesting. Learning the language and customs of the land is difficult enough when a person is working, finding new friends, and starting a family so far away from their own native land.

Born to a farmer in Hiroshima, Japan, he is the second son. Like Granduncle Nobujiro, not an heir to the family property, he must be always subservient to his father and oldest brother. This is the so-called code in Japan of that time.

He finishes high school and joins the Japanese Imperial Navy during the First World War. He was injured in an explosion aboard a ship and is in a coma. Since his father and mother both are in Los Angeles at this time, his oldest brother and other members of his family are told by the doctors that Father will not live much longer because of his head injury. Father must have heard this conversation between the doctor and family, because soon after, he disappears from the hospital. No one knows where Father is. Is he alive or dead?

After two years of disappearance, Father returns to the ancestral home in Hiroshima, Japan, letting everyone know that he is alive and well. His oldest brother, in 1967, tells me that Father spent two years in China during the 1920s. Many nations are in China in the 20's, trying to split up the country and claim some portion of it for themselves; a very troubling time before Japan runs rampant trying to conquer it all, then it becomes a living hell for China.

Nothing else is said, except that father loves to fish for ai for hours in the river that runs alongside the village. It is a kawa to them, which means river, but when I see this stream during the summer, it is a creek, but it must be a raging river during the monsoon season. Ai is a small fish, like a smelt or grunion, which is charcoal broiled to a crisp and eaten whole, starting from the head, and ending at the tail, which is also consumed, bones and all. I am visiting during my one-week R&R (rest and recreation) from the Viet Nam War in 1967. He gave me a liter of Sapporo Beer and a tumbler of sake. After the tasty lunch, we have a siesta. It was very easy for me to fall asleep after consuming all that beer and sake by myself.

Uncle walks me through the farmland and under a huge grape arbor covering a large area. I remember a story about a fox that eats grapes hanging from a grape arbor like this one. Naturally, the fox must leap many times to be rewarded with the large, juicy, ripe red grapes. Near this arbor is the school where my father attended. The school is a large two-story wooden structure painted white to protect it from the elements. It seems old, probably as old as these grapevines we are passing.

Beyond, we walk to a path leading up the side of the mountain with old growth of trees, mainly pine. The forest is dense, and the trees form a canopy over the path. This walk up a bit on the well-worn path tires me at the age of thirty- four, but Uncle, who is well over seventy years old, must wait for me to catch up with him. Here I am, attached to a Mobile Construction Battalion (Sea Bees) in Viet Nam, half his age, and I can't keep up with him, walking up the mountain path. Am I combat ready or what? Soon we reach the markers of some of our departed family members. I can't make out which marker belongs to whom, so Uncle points out the important ones that are Grandfather, Grandmother, Uncle etc. to me. Grandfather and Grandmother have their ashes brought from the United States and placed with their relatives. It is all carved out in stone in the Kanji style of Japanese writing.

There is an old photograph of Father in his suit, standing in front of a large city-block-long building, and on the reverse side, there is mention that this is in Berlin, where he spent four years. He never mentions this fact to anyone in the family until this photograph suddenly appears years after his death. Is he trying to tell us about his past by showing this photo now? Very mysterious indeed. What was he doing there during the heyday of Berlin in the 1920s?

He was injured on a ship about 1920, then spent two years in China and in Berlin for four years. This all happens when the world is experiencing a great change in these places. Well, Sam Saito is where the action is until he is about twenty-six years old - to 1925-26. What a colorful life to this point, but nothing ones mentioned or written about this period in his life.

My father told my wife, Naida, that he farmed in Mexico and in Otay near the Tijuana border in San Diego. This is mentioned while he is speaking Spanish to her. He speaks the language rather well. He farms lima beans using the dry farming method. That is, the soil is tilled just prior to the rainy season, and the beans planted. The rains will do the rest, provided there is adequate rainfall. The average rainfall in this region is nine to ten inches per year. After all, San Diego County is a desert. If there is a drought, the season will be a total failure. He didn't farm here for very long.

He asks whether the old back road to Tijuana is still there. Yes, it is still there. During the weekend, Father would get on his huge mule and ride it bareback to Tijuana. How do I know he rides horses and mules bareback? I have several pictures of him, and he never uses a saddle.

Tijuana is a wide-open town; yes, it is wide open, and he does say that marijuana is sold at the corner openly.

After drinking all night during the weekend in Tijuana, he would unhitch the mule, climb aboard, kick its side, and off they go back to the farm. The mule takes Father back to the farm while he sleeps on its huge back. Evidently, the mule has made many trips to Father's watering hole, and when the signal to return home to the mule's watering hole is given, he wastes no time at all to get there.

Father moves to the Los Angeles area about 1929 to be near his father and mother. Most immigrants leave their family and country to make a new life in America. Not my father, he left his country to be with his family in America. Uncle Seiki (Tom) mentions how he appreciates Father bringing him to America. Uncle Seiki said that one day, he was riding behind Father on a motorcycle, and they were talking away, enjoying the ride. At a stop, Father took off quickly and Uncle Seiki fell off the bike. Father just kept talking and driving down the road in Los Angeles, unaware of the incident. Uncle Seiki just laughs about it. This motorcycle must have been an Indian because he does mention how he loved his Indian bike. While in Los Angeles, Father works at a movie studio where Charles Chaplin acts.

About 1930, Father moves to Berryessa, California, near San Jose, to farm. He learns that there are two young ladies living in San Francisco whose parents came from Hiroshima, Japan. Actually, the parents' family home is across the river from the Saitos' ancestral home. Quickly, he introduces himself and later my mother and he get married. From this union, I come into this world in 1933, and later seven of my siblings join me. Now my father has Mother, me, and Granduncle Nobujiro living on the farm.

Since Asians cannot own any property in California during this time, Father is a tenant farmer or sharecropper. Since the Depression is still in its height, no one is making any money, not even farmers. A tenant farmer or sharecropper is at the mercy of landowner and buyers from canneries, packing and shipping companies. Father finally goes broke in the spring of 1938 and moves to San Jose, California and finds a full-time job as a janitor at Hale Brothers Department Store, several miles from our rented house.

Life is still difficult from 1938 to 1941. He manages to give us shelter, food, and clothing. What else can he do when there is a Depression going on in the United States? Father has a very large family to support, and he still takes us to eat at a Chinese restaurant less than one block away.

We all are placed in a concentration camp away from San Jose and Father is worried that we may get separated somewhere along the line. At our semipermanent home in Heart Mountain, Wyoming, Father shows his true colorful life, because he is now incarcerated but free to move around in camp. He shows that although this is a prison for him and the family, there are things he can do to make life more bearable and enjoyable for all at Sam's Place, a gambling room often serving sake when available.

There is a group picture of Father in the front row center, carrying a first aid kit with his right arm around a man. This was a photo to celebrate delivery of much needed soy sauce to the camp. Many barrels of Kikkoman soy sauce have dried, but some of it is salvaged by adding a little water to it. Was father carrying the first aid kit to signify that this delivery was by the Red Cross? The whole group is in front of a barracks and the picture is split at the roof line; the upper half shows the camp, looking toward Heart Mountain. Brother Ted is squatting in front extreme right, eating a chicken leg. I know that it is not egg foo yung, because he hates it. How can anyone hate as tasty a meal as egg foo yung? (This picture is not reprinted here because of copyright laws.)

After the war in 1945, Father and our family return to San Jose, California and he quickly starts working for Hale Brothers Department Store as a janitor. Many other Japanese work in the fields as laborers. These men, women, and children are all working to earn a living. Everyone who can work finds employment to start a new life after the war, many returning with several hundred dollars in their possession, but poor. They all look forward to a brighter future than they had a few months ago in camp.

Father gives Mother $1,000 one week before returning to San Jose. These are his savings from work and Sam's Place. He did not profit from making sake or from pickled vegetables, according to Mother. He started totally broke at the start of the war and it took him almost four years to accumulate $1,000. This is a sizeable amount of money that is used to get settled down, buying furniture, household goods, and an old pre-war sedan.

Not many Japanese have a car currently. Very few cars were built during the Second World War, and even old cars are hard to come by. Father had to paint his car bright yellow orange so everyone could see it coming down the street. Yes, everyone who saw him coming would let us know that he is coming. My face turns red. I don't know about my sisters, but it is a little embarrassing riding in this bright yellow-orange car. Soon, this embarrassment disappears, and we are going to picnics, parks, and even fishing in this old bright colored car that everyone could see for blocks ahead. Father is unique.

The Japanese people, some of them, think Father is working below his station, but he cares less, because he tells me that any kind of work that has to be done is not below a person's station, if it is morally correct and not a criminal activity. Later in life, after Father's demise, many people came to Mother and told her that Father had lent them hundreds of dollars to get them through a rough time. It sure wasn't below the borrower's station to ask for money from Father. This was during the time just several years after the war, when our family was trying to get out of living in basements.

During my high school year, Father came to me and asked if I could lend his boss, a janitorial contractor, $150. Naturally, I agree. Father has money to lend his boss, but he has lent him too much money that he said that was enough. The boss really has a serious gambling problem, and he spends most of his days at the union hall, gambling with his friends, paying no attention to business. Later, the boss could not pay his debts, so Father and he agreed to turn several accounts over to Father. This is the start of Sam's Janitorial Service, which has become a very lucrative business. He owns his own business within four years after leaving camp.

Father has seen many new inventions come into this world since he was born in 1899; he said there will be much more to come, and he would like to live to see these new changes that will affect all of us mostly for the good. He was really born before his time-driving around in a bright-colored car when most of the cars where painted black; giving me a car when I'm still in high school; encouraging everyone in the family to work during the summer for their own allowance, including clothing.

Although Father is in constant pain because of his arthritis, his complaints are minimal, because he consumes aspirin by the handful daily to ease the pain. When he is given cortisone by the hospital, his arthritis problem seems to disappear. His comment is that this is a true wonder drug, and he wishes that it was invented long ago. This is a steroid and harmful if used constantly, so the doctor did not use it for Father's arthritis.

My parents take a long trip to Japan to see how much it has changed. War always changes the landscape of any country. Father wants to visit many of Japan's onzen, mineral spas. As Japan is a volcanic nation, many of the islands are made from volcanic activity, and even to this date, earthquakes are constantly reminding the people that any one of their dormant volcanoes can awaken. The mineral spas have pain-relieving powers, and this is what Father wants to experience. I guess that the many mineral spas in California do not have pain-healing powers, because they never advertise it. He must be carried on board the airplane going to Japan, but after several months of visiting Japan and their many spas, Father walks off the plane unaided, with a beaming smile. Truly a miracle.

Father's love for Mother was so strong that when he is old and knowing that the time is close at hand, he asks Mother, "We sure had a wonderful life, didn't we?" Then later he tells my mother to have fun and take her time and not forget to visit the Grand Canyon, and don't worry about him, because he'll be waiting for her. When he passes, the nurse who was at his bedside tells my mother that father called out, "Mama."

My father never knew his mother very well because she passed away when he was young. His stepmother was not very close to Father either because she spent most of her life in Los Angeles. Father always called my mother "Mama." So, the last word my papa said was Mama, calling his wife who he loved so much.

Yayeko Saito
December 1913 - April 1999

Mother was born deaf in her left ear and with partial hearing in her right ear. She married at the very young age of eight, to a man who is a traditional conservative Japanese thirty-two years of age. A traditional conservative Japanese usually will seek out a spouse who is in perfect physical as well as mental health. They want genes to produce perfect children, and deafness is a physical flaw. The love bug bit both my parents; they quickly married and had many children who do not have hearing impairment.

Mother was born in a small town called Nicolas, California, north of Sacramento. She is sent to Hiroshima, Japan to be raised by her Russian grandmother. Mother has two older sisters, all born in the United States. Aunt Fujino was born in the territory of Hawaii, where my grandfather went with my grandmother to be a Japanese schoolteacher at a sugar plantation. They soon immigrate to California.

Mother's grandmother brings her to the first class at school and sits her in front. Grandmother tells her to listen very carefully and asks everyone to speak up because Mother is hard of hearing. Her grandmother must have taught Mother how to lip read, because I swear, she can hear us whispering at times.

She always tells us never to talk badly about other people, because their feelings will be hurt. How many times and for how many reasons have people hurt Mother's feelings?

During the winter, Mother's grandmother would give her a warm sweet potato and have her hold it while walking to school to keep warm. This sweet potato will be eaten later. Sweet potato is healthier than rice for a person, especially eating it with the skin and all. Rice is worth more to be sold at the market than sweet potatoes. Is this the reason that a country child is healthier than a city child?

There is a forest fire bearing down on the small village where Mother is living, and her grandmother digs a hole in the field to bury all the expensive clothes and valuables, so the fire will not destroy them. The fire dies out prior to getting to the village, much to the relief of the townspeople. Is this the reason valuables have been buried in the past, not only to protect them from fires but thieves as well?

Another disaster action Mother uses is to run into a bamboo patch during an earthquake. The root system of the bamboo is so thick that the earth could open under the patch but will not tear the roots apart, keeping her safe from harm. Remember now, run, and find a bamboo patch when there is an earthquake.

When Mother reaches the age of sixteen, she decides that she must return to the United States to be with her oldest sister, Fujino, living in San Francisco. There is a law that children born in the United States but moved to Japan or China must return prior to a certain age to be a citizen of the United States. I have not studied the law on this, but several older Japanese Americans, Kibei Nisei, a person born in the United States who went to Japan to be educated and then returned and spoke to me about this law.

Mother boards a ship bound for San Francisco, and from day one, she is seasick, not being able to keep food or liquid in her system. This may be from her deafness, where the inner ear is unable to keep balance from the ship's movement riding the sea waves. Finally, reaching Honolulu, Mother debarks and immediately is well.

She meets a local banana salesperson and falls in love with him. This is what we call a teenage crush, but to her, the passion was so great that Mother buys a whole stalk of ripe bananas and has it delivered to her cabin. Mother eats a lot of bananas and regains some of her energy.

When the steamer leaves port and sails east to California, Mother immediately loses the bananas she had consumed and suffers seasickness until landing in San Francisco. She must have looked a sight to her oldest sister. Mother is only four feet eleven inches tall and must have been light as a feather. She never told me how she left the ship, but I bet she was the happiest person alive to debark that steamer.

Mother works as a housemaid for a local doctor to supplement the family earning. The money earned from farming is not enough. It appears that the family really suffered during the Depression, but I cannot remember any day that we went without food. There is a picture of me wearing shoes, sitting on the running board of a milk truck with a bottle in my arms. Even the clothes I am wearing appear to be in very good condition. There are other pictures of the family members wearing shoes States who went to Japan to be educated and then returned and spoke to me about this law. Mother boards a ship bound for San Francisco, and from day one, she is seasick, not being able to keep food or liquid in her system. This may be from her deafness, where the inner ear is unable to keep balance from the ship's movement riding the sea waves. Finally, reaching Honolulu, Mother debarks and immediately is well.

She meets a local banana salesperson and falls in love with him. This is what we call a teenage crush, but to her, the passion was so great that Mother buys a whole stalk of ripe bananas and has it delivered to her cabin. Mother eats a lot of bananas and regains some of her energy.

When the steamer leaves port and sails east to California, Mother immediately loses the bananas she had consumed and suffers seasickness until landing in San Francisco. She must have looked a sight to her oldest sister. Mother is only four feet eleven inches tall and must have been light as a feather. She never told me how she left the ship, but I bet she was the happiest person alive to debark that steamer.

Mother works as a housemaid for a local doctor to supplement the family earning. The money earned from farming is not enough. It appears that the family really suffered during the Depression, but I cannot remember any day that we went without food. There is a picture of me wearing shoes, sitting on the running board of a milk truck with a bottle in my arms. Even the clothes I am wearing appear to be in very good condition. There are other pictures of the family members wearing shoes hall personnel take care of all of that. All the worry about the next meal planning and buying is gone. Mother now devotes much of her time caring for the younger children and keeping us clean, as well as our clothes. Mother tells me that camp is an easy lifestyle, and it sure does beat cooking.

At Heart Mountain, Wyoming, Mother keeps all of us busy by having everyone participate in keeping the barrack rooms clean, and the cast iron potbellied stove always fired up. The small coal bin is always kept full by us children. The girls help wash all the clothes and hang them to dry near the stove. Since she has much more time on her hands, unlike living in that Stone Age house at San Jose, Mother finds friends and joins a very large sewing class. She gets her health back and teaches us how to ice skate, swim, and go on picnics to the river but not to swim there.

Many of my friends who have heard my story probably think that I am exaggerating or lying when I tell them of my experience through my immediate family, who are now far beyond where we all will eventually be. I have not actually been there beyond; however, my dear mother and youngest brother have expressed through their words or actions that there is a beyond and the soul travels there upon death.

In 1998 and 1999, my mother was in the hospital many times from heart attacks. Her heart keeps missing a beat, indicating she has a poor heart. Finally, Mother just did not want to be hooked up to any machine to keep her alive and made her wishes known that she wanted to go home and be in hospice care. A family friend by the name of Eddie lived at my sister Mary's home under hospice care because he had less than six months left to live. The cancer is eating away from his lungs. My mother and sister will attend to him until he expires. His passing is pain free and he appreciates the excellent care taken by Mother, Mary, and the hospice personnel to make everything comfortable.

Mother knows how painful and how much agony there is when a person has cancer, but seeing a contented Eddie during his last days, she believes that hospice care is the way to go, especially the care given at home by loved ones. Mother is happy being at home in Mary's loving care instead of the hospital, where she was very uncomfortable in a strange environment. She knows that her passing will be pain-free and comfortable, with her daughter Mary and family around her.

I'm holding her hand and wrist while her pulse is felt with the missing heartbeats, then there is no pulse for the longest time. Instead of panicking and telling the rest of the family who are gathered in the kitchen and dinette, I pray for her soul to enter heaven to be with father and the rest of her family. After what appears to be many minutes, the pulse returns.

During this time, my brother Ted cannot call out on his phone, so he takes his cell phone outdoors and still cannot get a line out. The house phone does not have a dial tone. No communications are allowed in or out of the house currently. The bombers are bombing Bosnia, and the war is on, according to the television.

Mother opens her eyes, sees me, and asks, *"Who are you?"*

"This is Bobby!" I reply.

Then she tells me, *"I was there but they didn't want me yet, so they sent me back."*

"Who sent you back? Was it the angels?" I asked. *"Yes, it was the angels. The telephone is not working. There's a big war going on,"* she says.

How did my mother know that the telephones were not working in the house and there is a war in Bosnia? My mother is totally deaf in one ear and hearing impaired in the right ear. This is her birth defect. With a hearing aid, she is able to hear. She was not wearing the hearing aid, and I had to speak loudly in her right ear for her to understand what I'm saying.

Yes, Mother went beyond and returned to let me know that there is a beyond. Right away, I will explain to the family members what has happened. I wonder if they believe what has happened to Mother. Later, Mother could not remember what had transpired, so I did not press it further. She has other problems that need to be confronted, step by step, day by day.

She passes on March 14, 1999, which is my brother Ted's birthday. Ted is by her side, and he said that her last words were, *"Happy birthday, Ted."* I went to Israel and the West Bank (Jerusalem) and prayed for her soul.

My brother Julian has a massive heart attack and calls 911. When the paramedics came, his heart had stopped, but the paramedics kept working on him until they reached the emergency ward. The doctors tell the family (Ted first) that Julian's heart has stopped for a very long time, and he may be brain damaged. His heart and lungs are now working with the aid of the life support system.

His daughter, Heather, asks to have the life support going because she wants Julian to have a chance to survive the heart attack. Julian fought to have Mother's life support going, and she survived that heart attack. After knowing how hard Julian fought for Mother's life, Heather had to do the same for her dad. Julian's situation is different, in that his brain has no activity, and without life support, his organs will just shut down immediately.

Many of the family members go to his bedside to bid him goodbye, including his two ex-wives. We all love him and do not want to see him die, but the doctors all recommend that the life support systems be removed, because Julian has no brain activity and if he happens to survive the removal of the life support system, he will be a vegetable. The doctors are sure that he will expire as soon as the support systems are removed.

Heather gives the doctors permission to remove the life support system. The doctor recommends that we all go home, and he will call to inform us of the time Julian expires.

We are all on the road going home, when at 10:35 am, May 30, 2003, Mary with a clinched fist thumps her breast. I asked, "What's wrong?" and she replies, "Nothing." I said, "Don't do that." I normally would not talk to Mary like that, but I was concerned. At that time, Heather calls Mary on the cell phone that her car was bouncing up and down on the freeway like Julian was jumping on it, and that Heather's baby, Jade, woke up and pointed skyward and said, "Bye, Grandpa." All witnessed by Heather, Pam her mother, and young son Dylan.

At 10:40 am, Mary receives a call on her cell phone from the doctor and he said Julian expired peacefully about five minutes ago. The doctor said that he could not get a hold of Heather because the line was busy. Heather and Mary were talking to each other about the bouncing car and Jade's *"Bye, Grandpa."*

Julian visited Jade at the time of his passing. He loves his granddaughter Jade and wants to say goodbye to Jade, Heather, Dylan, Pam his ex-wife, and sister Mary.

Like Mother dying on her son Ted's birthday, Julian dies on his daughter Heather's birthday. Both have expressed in their own way that there is a beyond.

A haiku poem

Singing Frog (Kairu)

I heard a frog sing

Happily calling me home

O kairu kairu

Mom loves frogs (*kairu*) and has a few figurines of them. Kairu also means "going home" in Japanese. On New Year's night, January 2003, a frog is singing as my siblings are leaving Mary's house after a day of feasting our traditional New Year's meal. The frog is on the corner eave of the house nearest the walkway from the main entrance. How can a frog leap ten feet up into the air and land on the roof of a house? Mother came back as a frog that night to sing her New Year's blessing to us. Buddhists believe in reincarnation, especially to animals.

www.ingramcontent.com/pod-product-compliance
Lightning Source LLC
LaVergne TN
LVHW040146080526
838202LV00042B/3043